Test taker characteristics and test performance: A structural modeling approach

STUDIES IN LANGUAGE TESTING...2
Series editor: Michael Milanovic

Also in this series:

An investigation into the comparability of two tests of English as a foreign language: The Cambridge-TOEFL comparability study
Lyle F. Bachman, F. Davidson, K. Ryan, I-C Choi

Performance testing, cognition and assessment: Selected papers from the 15th Language Testing Research Colloquium (LTRC) Cambridge and Arnhem, 1993

Test taker characteristics and test performance: A structural modeling approach

Antony John Kunnan

California State University, Los Angeles

CAMBRIDGE
UNIVERSITY PRESS

Published by the Press Syndicate of the University of Cambridge
The Pitt Building, Trumpington Street, Cambridge CB2 1RP
40 West 20th Street, New York, NY 10011, USA
10 Stamford Road, Oakleigh, Melbourne 3166, Australia

First published 1995

Printed in Great Britain at the University Press, Cambridge

British Library cataloguing in publication data

University of Cambridge, Local Examinations Syndicate
Test taker characteristics and test performance: A structural modeling
approach

Antony John Kunnan

1. Education. Assessment 2. Education. Tests. Setting

ISBN   0 521 481 68 6 hard cover
          0 521 484 66 9 paperback

Contents

Series Editor's note   VII
Preface   IX

Chapter 1   Introduction   1

Context of the problem   1
Model formulation and construct validation   2
Modeling in language testing   5
Purpose   6
Significance   7
Definition of terms   8
Limitations   9

Chapter 2   Theoretical models and empirical studies   11

Theoretical models   11
Empirical studies   15
Structural modeling   19
Summary   23

Chapter 3   The structural modeling approach and   24
**   its application to this study**

Overview   24
Data   24
Structural modeling   28
Preliminary analysis   32
Research questions   42
Structural models   44

Chapter 4   Modeling the data: The results of the study   48

Overview   48
Modeling test taker characteristics   48
Modeling test performance   51
Test taker characteristics and test performance factors   57
Model 1   57

Model 2 62
Alternative models 70
Summary 71

Chapter 5 Discussion of results and conclusions **72**

Overview 72
Influence of previous exposure 72
Influence of and on monitoring 75
EFL test performance 75
Model comparisons 77
Conclusions 78
Final thoughts 81

Appendices **83**
References **127**
Subject Index **138**
Author Index **141**

Series Editor's note

This is the second volume in the series Studies in Language Testing, and is based on data collected during work carried out for the first volume *An investigation into the comparability of two tests of English as a foreign language* (1995). Antony Kunnan was involved in this project and used some of the additional data collected to write a doctoral dissertation under the supervision of Lyle Bachman, at the University of California, Los Angeles. This volume is essentially a lightly edited version of that dissertation. It has been published in this series because it represents a significant piece of research, related to the work being done in Cambridge, and of relevance to those involved in language testing. It is unfortunately often the case that work of this kind is never seen by more than a very few people. However, this volume documents effectively a complex approach to construct validation that has aroused some interest in recent years. It can serve as a useful overview with worked examples for those interested in the use of structural modeling in the construct validation of language tests.

Although much data on test taker characteristics was collected during the study that led to Volume 1 in this series, only a limited amount was reported on, with Chapter 5 investigating the effects of test preparation on test performance through the use of regression analyses and the Mantel-Haenszel procedure. Kunnan has taken the research further and he looks at the relationships between previous exposure to English both at home and abroad, motivation and monitoring and performance on various components of the First Certificate in English (FCE) produced by Cambridge, and the Test of English as a Foreign Language (TOEFL), produced by ETS. Kunnan uses a structural modeling approach, which, although complex, allows for the hypothesised relationships among constructs as well as between constructs and observed variables to be represented.

Since *An investigation into the comparability of two tests of English as a foreign language* was carried out in 1988, Cambridge has continued to work on and sponsor research that attempts to better understand the relationships between candidate characteristics and performance with a view to improving the quality of Cambridge examinations and, in a broader sense, contributing to second language acquisition research. A bank of questionnaire items has been developed and trialled and is in the process of being validated at the time of writing. This process is taking place both under the direction of Lyle Bachman at the

University of California, and under my supervision in Cambridge. The bank has items in two main areas which focus on a total of seven subcategories as follows:

Area 1   Socio-Psychological Factors
1   Attitudes
2   Motivation
3   Anxiety
4   Effort

Area 2   Strategic Factors
5   Cognitive Strategies
6   Metacognitive Strategies
7   Communication Strategies
It is anticipated that this work will be published in the series in 1997.

To conclude, I would like to express Cambridge's thanks to Antony Kunnan for this work which is an important contribution to the Studies in Language Testing Series.

Michael Milanovic
Cambridge, June 1995

Preface

This study is a slightly revised version of my doctoral dissertation submitted to the University of California, Los Angeles, in December 1991. My interest in the topic area of test taker characteristics, test performance and construct validation began with my association with the Cambridge-TOEFL comparability study, directed by Professor Lyle Bachman. It was during this time I became interested in factor analytic and structural modeling techniques. Bringing these two aspects together under the umbrella of construct validation research was my major task. Needless to say, I would have achieved much less if it was not for the many professors and researchers who helped me in my attempt.

I wish to express my gratitude and my indebtedness to Lyle Bachman of UCLA for generously giving me and this project hundreds of hours of his precious time, for insightful discussions on language testing issues, for reviews on earlier drafts of my manuscript, and for financial support for the projects.

I also want to acknowledge others who gave generously in different ways towards the project: Professor John Schumann for raising appropriate ontological and epistemological issues in SLA and language testing research, Professors Bengt Muthen and Peter Bentler for technical advice and methodological strategies on structural modeling, and other UCLA colleagues and language testing researchers who were often the best critics: Brian Lynch, Fred Davidson, Miyuki Sasaki, Toru Kinoshita, Patsy Duff, Sally Jacoby, Sara Cushing, Jim Purpura, Helen George and Maureen Mason. Of course, none of these people is to be held responsible for any errors or points of view that are found in this study.

Finally, I would like to thank Michael Milanovic of UCLES for his encouragement from the start of the project to now when the project is being published under his editorship, and Helen Goring for her patience and attention to detail during the publication process.

As always, I am grateful to my wife, Suchi, for her assistance in many ways, too numerous to list here.

Antony John Kunnan
Pasadena, California
March 1994

1 Introduction

Context of the problem

A recent concern among researchers in the field of language testing has been the identification and characterization of the individual characteristics that influence performance on tests of English as a foreign language (EFL) or English as a second language (ESL). One group of characteristics that has been identified and characterized to some extent is what is broadly called test taker characteristics (TTCs) or background characteristics (Bachman 1990). These test taker characteristics include personal characteristics or attributes such as age, native language and culture, and gender, educational characteristics such as background knowledge, previous instruction or exposure to English, as well as cognitive, psychological and social characteristics such as learning strategies and styles, attitude and motivation, aptitude and intelligence, field dependence and independence, extroversion and introversion, and anxiety, personality, and risk-taking.

Research on several of these characteristics or factors from the perspective of second language acquisition has shown that some of these influence language learning to differing degrees (Gardner 1985, 1988). However, from the perspective of language testing, the influence of these characteristics has not been given sufficient attention, although research in this area could contribute directly to the construction of a theory of construct validity of EFL test performance.

The goal of this study, therefore, was to investigate and explore the influence of some of these test taker characteristics on EFL test performance and in doing so, hopefully, to contribute towards a theory of construct validation for EFL test performance. Methodologically, this study used a structural modeling approach developed in the 1970s. Structural modeling involves the formulation of models by positing relationships among constructs, like those based on test taker characteristics and EFL test performance variables, evaluation of these models, and if the models do not adequately explain the relationships, the proposing of alternative substantive models, evaluation of these and so on. Thus, model formulation and evaluation as a way of exploring the structure of the relationships formed the crux of this study. This did not mean the method used was unfocused empiricism for its own sake. Rather, it followed, in the words of Cronbach (1989), not a "strong program of construct validation" which involves formal hypothesis-testing but "a weak program of construct validation" which involves widespread support for explanations from many perspectives.

It was this researcher's hope, then, that this study, while not aspiring to provide any definitive answers to the research questions, would suggest the direction for a program of research that would focus not on confirming or rejecting a set of hypotheses but instead on seeking explanations for the phenomena that were being investigated. Cronbach (1989:165) puts this approach best when he states that

> *the investigation should aim to illuminate the test and the related*
> *construction so that persons making decisions see more clearly*
> *how to use the test, and those pursuing research know where the*
> *greatest perplexities lie.*

Model formulation and construct validation

Model formulation and evaluation of the structure of psychological and educational tests (or structural modeling) have been inextricably tied to the concept of construct validation. Construct validation, which began as an alternative to content analysis, criterion validity and predictive power, has evolved over the last four decades and has now taken centre stage (Messick 1989). In the 1950s, the concept was understood as the strict "nomological network" as proposed by Cronbach and Meehl (1955) and with the dominating influence of logical empiricists like Wittgenstein (1922), Ayer (1936) and Popper (1962), models were strictly formulated with hypotheses or had a convergent and discriminant validation emphasis (Campbell and Fiske 1959).

As formulated by the American Psychological Association Committee on Psychological Tests (1954) and introduced formally by Cronbach and Meehl (1955:283), a construct was defined as "a postulated attribute of people, assumed to be reflected in test performance" and it was proposed that tests should be evaluated with regard to data such as group differences, correlational results and internal structure of tests. This emphasis on construct, according to Bentler (1978:288), "represented an important attempt to make substantive theory relevant to the typical process of test construction and evaluation". Messick (1980:1015) characterizes construct validation in a similar vein:

> *Construct validity is indeed the unifying concept that integrates*
> *criterion and content considerations into a common framework*
> *for testing rational hypotheses about theoretically relevant*
> *relationships.*

But many researchers found several aspects of the Cronbach-Meehl proposal to be vague and unclear: Loevinger (1957) was dissatisfied with the term "construct" and suggested the use of the term "traits" while Bechtold (1959) objected to the concept as well as the implementation. Bentler (1978:288) states that "the value of the concept has remained a source of some contention (Campbell 1960; Cronbach 1971)" and he argues that

> *one major source of confusion regarding the concept of construct validation and its possible contribution to social sciences lies in the difficulties associated with operationalizing the procedure. If a more concrete methodology to implement the concept could be devised, many of the controversies surrounding the idea might be eliminated.*

In order to remedy this situation, Bentler (1978:289) proposed a causal-modeling approach to construct validation, extending the Cronbach-Meehl framework by going beyond the traditional primary focus. Bentler states that this approach would be

> *concerned with the construct validity of a substantive theory, focusing immediate attention on the entire nomological network of associations of a given construct to other constructs and manifest variables.*

Though Bentler's proposal was new at the time, his use of the central notion of "nomological network" was an echo of the Cronbach and Meehl (1955:23) approach: "To validate a claim that a test measures a construct, a nomological net surrounding the concept must exist".

Over the last decade, however, the central focus of the concept of construct validation has changed. Messick (1989:23) summarizes the shift in focus, thus,

> *Indeed, descriptions of construct validity in terms of nomological networks still occur in the present chapter, as they did in precursors to it ... but no longer as a requirement or defining feature of construct validation. Nomological networks are viewed as an illuminating way of speaking systematically about the role of constructs in psychological theory and measurement, but not as the only way. The nomological framework offers a useful guide for disciplined thinking about the process of validation to the exclusion of other approaches such as causal explanation or the modeling of operative mechanisms.*

Messick (1989:48) also proposes a distinction between "nomological validity" and "nomothetic span", a term made popular by Embretson (1983). Nomothetic span, in Messick's words,

> *refers to the empirical network of relationships of the test to measures of other constructs and criterion behaviors. Technically speaking, nomothetic span is broader than nomological validity as ordinarily conceived because it explicitly includes correlations of the test with other measures of the same construct and with*

> *other measures of the same construct obtained under different conditions.*

Embretson (1983) offers more detail in her characterization of nomothetic span; she includes multiple measures of each construct as well as targeted predictive relationships between the test and specific criterion behaviors. In this way, criterion related evidence is subsumed under the umbrella of construct validation. Embretson's nomothetic span also indicates the predictive importance of the test as a measure of individual differences.

Messick (1989:48–9) sums up the value of using the nomothetic span concept:

> *The stronger and more frequent the test's correlations with other variables that should correlate with the construct on theoretical grounds, the wider the nomothetic span. Furthermore, if the constructs operative in test performance have been previously identified in the construct representation phase, quantitative models that permit a priori construct specification may be applied to the correlational data. For example, path-analytic or structural models (Bentler 1980; James et al., 1982; Joreskog & Sorbom, 1979) may be used to appraise the extent to which the component constructs can account for the test's external pattern of relationships.*

From a philosophical perspective too, the construct validation "method of inquiry" suggested by the nomothetic span fits well with the Kantian inquiry system. The Kantian system, as put forth by Churchman (1971), entails the formulation or identification of alternative perspectives on a theory or problem representation which explicitly recognizes the strong intertwining of theory and data. Messick (1989) states that "a Kantian inquiry system starts with at least two alternative theories ... from each are developed corresponding alternative data sets or fact networks. Contrariwise, the Kantian approach might begin with an existing fact network, for which alternative theories are then formulated" (p. 31). The hope of this approach is that from one of the multiple alternative theories, one or several may be identified as best in one or several senses. Once again as Messick (1989:31) puts it:

> *The standard of validity for a Kantian inquiry system is the goodness of fit or match between the theory and its associated data. The Kantian approach is suitable for moderately ill-structured problems, where diverse perspectives need to be examined in order to be able to conceptualize the issues, as in dealing with a complex social problem such as alcoholism or a complex theoretical problem such as the nature of achievement motivation.*

Churchman (1971:177) compares the Kantian with the Lockean inquirer In this manner:

> *The Lockean inquirer displays the "fundamental" data that all experts agree are accurate and relevant, and then builds a consistent story out of these. The Kantian inquirer displays the same story from different points of view, emphasizing thereby that what is put into the story by the internal mode of representation is not given from the outside.*

Recent papers that have followed the Kantian perspective, Quine's (1953) arguments against hypothesis-testing and Feyerabend's (1975, 1981) methodological pluralism in the field of second language acquisition include Schumann's (1993) case for exploration instead of hypothesis-testing and falsification and Van Lier's (in press) arguments for pursuing understanding in different ways.

Modeling in language testing

While modeling or structural modeling in language testing is not new, it was only in the late 1970s that language testers began to posit theories of language proficiency and test them. The focus of these and other researchers has been rather specific: they investigated the "components", "traits" or "factors" of language proficiency (Oller 1979; Oller and Hinofotis 1980; Hinofotis 1983; Sang *et al.* 1986; Boldt 1988; Hale *et al.* 1989) and convergent and discriminant validation through the multitrait–multimethod matrix approach (Bachman and Palmer 1981). These researchers generally followed the Cronbach and Meehl (1955) framework of construct validation through the strong form of "causal modeling", the defining feature of which is a "nomological network".

It was only in 1990 that a more comprehensive and unified model of language test performance was put forward by Bachman (1990) who posited that four categories of influences on test scores are communicative language ability, test method facets, personal attributes or test taker characteristics, and random measurement error. This formulation provides a framework for an empirical investigation of a network of relationships which can finally relate the four categories that influence test performance.

This present study used this framework to investigate the relationships among test taker characteristics and test performance in order that this investigation can contribute to a theory of construct validation of EFL test performance. Messick (1989) and Embretson (1983) call this kind of construct validation process a "nomothetic span". Skehan (1991) characterizes this as typical of the kind of individual difference research in second language learning which is "to study individuals through constant categories that apply to everyone" (p. 293). Once again, philosophically, this expanded approach to construct validation is similar to the Kantian method of inquiry that is capable of dealing with complex social problems.

As Cronbach (1989:155) counsels, while discussing French's (1965) exposition of the Achilles' heel of factor analysis:

> *The explanation of a test performance depends on the respondent's process or style. Therefore, no one explanation for a test score is adequate. We will have to accept the viability of alternative explanations, and then will need to explain why the person uses one process rather than another.*

Perhaps, in the coming decades, advances in cognitive psychology and information-processing will suggest directions for research in test taker strategies and styles, an area not addressed in this study. And, perhaps, then, language learning and testing research might become idiographic in style, that is, in Skehan's (1991) words, a research approach which believes that "the individual can only be understood as an individual, without the straitjacket of other people's categories" (p. 293). Even if it does, the concept of "nomothetic span" through structural modeling could provide the necessary theoretical base for investigations of construct validation of tests and test performance so that idiographic style research could be supplemented adequately.

Purpose

This study investigated and explored the influences of test taker characteristics on EFL test performance by using a structural modeling approach. The specific purpose was to provide empirical evidence from a nomothetic span perspective for the factors that influence test performance. A clarification should focus this point: in any test situation (including the language test situation), there are test takers and tests. Test takers (in ESL/EFL) come to the test setting with certain personal attributes or background characteristics that may have a critical influence on their performance in the tests, in addition to the influence exerted by their language abilities. Thus, there is a nomothetic span, a set of structural relationships, in language testing that contributes to test taker performance which in turn impacts on the construct validation of tests.

Specifically, this study posited several models regarding the structure of certain test taker characteristics and EFL proficiency tests and the influences of these test taker characteristics on EFL test performance. These models were based on substantive theories in language testing and second language acquisition, and on preliminary exploratory factor analyses. Then, these relationships were explored and satisfactory explanations of fit of models to data were sought. In addition, the study investigated the extent to which similar models fit data from different groups based on native language, such as two native language family groups, Indo-European and non Indo-European. The general research question was: What are the relationships among test taker characteristics and test performance on EFL proficiency tests?

Significance

This study can contribute to the field of language testing and second language acquisition in theoretical, methodological and practical ways. First, although previous studies in second language acquisition have investigated the relationships among some test taker characteristics and language achievement (Gardner 1985), only a few studies (Stansfield and Hansen 1983; Hansen and Stansfield 1984; Fouly 1985; Chapelle 1988) with relatively few variables have investigated these relationships from the language testing perspective. The results of this study can, therefore, inform language test developers and researchers regarding the factors that influence test performance, and, therefore, about the validity of the theoretical underpinnings that inform these language tests. Bachman (1990:166) writes about this very concern:

> *A major concern in the design and development of language tests ... is to minimize the effects of test method, personal attributes, that are not part of the language ability, and random factors on test performance.*

In addition, in terms of construct validation research, this study used test taker characteristics as well as test performance data, unlike many previous studies in language testing that have investigated the construct validation of tests based solely on test performance (Bachman and Palmer 1981), with the exception of the few studies mentioned earlier (Stansfield and Hansen 1983; Hansen and Stansfield 1984; Fouly 1985; Chapelle 1988).

Methodologically, the study's use of a greater variety of EFL tests (10 in all) and a much more heterogenous population (from eight countries) than Gardner (1985) or Fouly (1985) increased the challenge and made this an interesting research study. In addition, structural modeling with EQS, which is a new statistical software for structural modeling (instead of LISREL, which has been the preferred software with language testing researchers), can provide us the opportunity to examine the software for future research in the field.

In addition to the theoretical and methodological significance, this study can provide useful insights for language testing practitioners. For example, significant structural relationships between test taker characteristics and test performance for the different groups (non Indo-European and Indo-European) can inform test users and test developers as well as language and curriculum developers and language teaching materials writers.

Definition of terms

Theoretical definitions of terms frequently used in the present study are given below:

Test taker characteristics

Bachman (1990) has characterized test taker characteristics, or personal attributes, as one of the four factors that affect language test scores or sources of variation in language test scores. These characteristics are made up of, in Bachman's list of sources, "cultural background, background knowledge, cognitive abilities, sex, and age" (1990:350). The three other factors or sources are communicative language ability, test method facets, and random factors.

In addition to the characteristics mentioned by Bachman, four kinds of characteristics have been discussed in the SLA literature:

1 **previous exposure to English** obtained through formal and/or informal exposure **in their home country**; and
2 **previous exposure to English** obtained through formal and/or informal exposure **in an English speaking country** (if they visited such a country); and
3 **motivation orientation to learn English**, whether this was instrumental or integrative (Gardner and Lambert 1972); and
4 **monitoring** (Krashen 1985) their own speaking and writing for English language errors as well as monitoring other people's English language errors.

Language proficiency

Language proficiency has been defined in many ways: from early frameworks like the skills and components model by Lado (1961) and Carroll (1961, 1968) to the context of discourse and situation models by Halliday and Hasan (1976) and Hymes (1972, 1973) and more recently to Canale and Swain (1980). Based on the last study, Bachman (1990) proposed a communicative language ability (CLA) model of language proficiency.

From these definitions, a language proficiency test can be operationally defined in this way: if a test developer uses the skills and components model, the proficiency test could reflect those components, and the language proficiency tests under development would focus on skills and components; on the other hand, if a test developer uses Bachman's communicative language ability model, the proficiency test could reflect the components of the communicative language ability model, and the language proficiency tests under development would focus on the three communicative language ability components. At this point in language testing research, however, it is an empirical question as to whether patterns of test performance conform to these operational definitions.

In this study, the EFL proficiency tests are broadly based on the skills and components model. The tests are organized basically into reading, writing, listening, and speaking skills. The tests are: the First Certificate in English (FCE), papers 1 to 5, developed and administered by the University of Cambridge Local Examinations Syndicate (UCLES 1987), the Test of English as a Foreign Language (TOEFL), parts 1 to 3, and the SPEAK, which are the retired forms of the Test of Spoken English (TSE) both developed and administered by the Educational Testing Service (ETS), and the Test of English Writing (TEW), developed and administered by the Cambridge-TOEFL Comparability Study researchers (Bachman *et al.* 1995).

Structural modeling

Structural modeling or structural equation modeling is a way of representing hypothesized relationships between constructs and observed variables and among constructs based on substantive theory or previous empirical research. In this approach, in brief, specific models are defined by sets of equations relating variables and constructs and these models are empirically tested. The terms structural or "causal" are generally used interchangeably but in this study "structural" will be preferred, as the term "causal", as in causal modeling, is inappropriate for this study. This is especially true because the purpose of this study is not to find causes for certain phenomena but rather to seek explanations for certain structural relationships.

EQS

EQS (pronounced like the letter "X") is a structural equations statistical software program developed by Bentler (1989) for multivariate structural modeling analysis. This program implements a general mathematical and statistical approach that helps researchers conduct linear structural modeling.

Limitations

There are several limitations on the scope of this study. The results of the study are of limited generalizability in many areas. First, the issue of population generalizability: the subjects for the study were adult non-native speakers of English from eight countries – Brazil, Egypt, France, Hong Kong, Japan, Spain, Thailand and Switzerland – the results, therefore, should only be generalized to individuals who have had similar background characteristics and performance. The results should not be generalized, for example, to children learning English in a bilingual program in the US.

Second, ecological generalizability: the results of this study should only be generalized to those countries with similar native languages and cultural settings. The results might be invalid across native languages and cultural settings.

Third, temporal generalizability: the results of this study should not be generalized beyond the present time, as the individual abilities could change because the status of English could be different in those countries as time goes by, and in turn, access to English could differ. Thus, these results might be invalid across time.

Finally, task generalizability: as this study used ten EFL tests with thirteen scores that were administered in 1988, the results of the study should not be generalized beyond the specific tests. This is because statistical test equating procedures with subsequent forms are rigorously followed only for the TOEFL and the SPEAK tests and not for the FCE and the TEW (which was developed only for the project). In addition, the 45-item questionnaire that was used for this study is not comprehensive. It does not include all the test taker characteristics that could be self-reported through a questionnaire. For example, several cognitive, psychological and social factors that were not used in the study include attitude, anxiety, aptitude, field dependence/independence, extroversion/introversion, intelligence, learning strategies and styles, personality and risk-taking.

Beyond generalizability, there is a critical methodological limitation: the structural models posited in the present study were neither exhaustive nor comprehensive. The models posited were based on current research in language testing and second language acquisition as well as some relationships suggested by the data which were within the scope of the current theories. But since a very large number of alternative structural models other than the ones used in this study could be posited, the fit or lack of fit of the specific models examined in this study does not mean that the models posited were the only ones that could satisfactorily explain the data. Furthermore, since this study was an exploratory one and therefore used model modification as a technique to improve model fit, this study did not seek to confirm or reject models. New data with similar models would be required for the confirmation or rejection of relationships found in this study.

2 Theoretical models and empirical studies

This chapter presents theoretical models and empirical studies of language test performance and second language acquisition by both language testing and SLA researchers that are relevant to this study. It also briefly discusses the features of structural modeling and an illustrative modeling study from the field of second language acquisition. The description of the theoretical models is presented first followed by an examination of the empirical studies. The chapter concludes with the illustrative modeling study.

Theoretical models

Factors that influence language test performance

Though considerable research in language testing has focused on construct validation, there is sufficient indication that research needs to focus on the factors that influence language test performance in order to achieve more informed construct validation results. Some studies have begun to show that several types of factors influence language test performance, but none of these studies has proposed a single over-arching model that could be used to investigate the effect of all these factors on language test performance.

Bachman's (1990:348) general model for explaining performance on language tests does just that; it provides a unified model that researchers can use to posit different hypotheses or relationships about factors that influence language test performance. Bachman states:

> *The four categories of influences on test scores included in this model are communicative language ability, test method facets, personal characteristics and random measurement error.*

The first category of influence in Bachman's terms is communicative language ability. In the words of Canale (1988), Bachman's communicative language ability has been developed on "extensive second-language teaching experience of its proponents, reviews of theories of communicative competence, and state-of-the-art empirical and measurement techniques" (p.68). Specifically, communicative language ability builds on the research in communicative competence by Canale and Swain (1980), Canale (1983) and others (Hymes 1972; Munby 1978; Widdowson 1978) and provides an ability-oriented definition of test content. Communicative language ability has three components, language competence, strategic competence, and psychophysiological mechanisms.

1 **language competence** is defined as "a set of specific knowledge components that are utilized in communication via language" (Bachman 1990, p.84). It is divided into two sub-components: organizational competence and pragmatic competence, both of which have further classifications. While organizational competence is concerned with the formal aspects of language like grammatical competence (morphology, phonology/orthography, syntax and vocabulary) and textual competence (cohesion and rhetorical organization), pragmatic competence is concerned with the functional aspects of language like illocutionary competence and sociolinguistic competence;

2 **strategic competence** is defined as "the mental capacity for implementing the components of language competence in contextualized communicative language use" (Bachman 1990, p.84). This competence involves processes in language use: assessment, planning and execution;

3 **the psychophysiological component** is defined as "the neurological and psychological processes involved in the actual execution of language as a physical phenomenon" (Bachman 1990, p.84).

This model, therefore, differs significantly from earlier conceptualizations of language ability which characterized language ability as skills and components (listening, speaking, reading and writing, and associated with these skills phonology-orthography, lexis, grammar and mechanics) as proposed by researchers like Lado (1961), Carroll (1968), Cooper (1968) and Harris (1969).

The second category of influence is test method facets. Briefly, test method facets include:

1 **characteristics of the testing environment,** which includes place and equipment, personnel, time of testing and physical conditions;

2 **characteristics of the test rubric,** which includes test organization in terms of salience, sequence and relative importance of parts, time allocation, scoring procedures, criteria for correctness and explicitness of procedures, and instructions in terms of language and channel used as well as specification of procedures and tasks;

3 **characteristics of the test input,** which includes format of the test in terms of channel, mode, form, vehicle and language of presentation, identification of problem, degree of speededness, language of the input in terms of length, organizational characteristics like grammar, cohesion and rhetorical organization, pragmatic characteristics like propositional content mainly in terms of vocabulary, degree of contextualization, distribution of new information and type of information, topic, genre and functions and sociolinguistic characteristics;

4 **characteristics of the expected response,** which include all the characteristics mentioned in 3;

5 **restrictions on response**; and
6 **relationship between input and response** in terms of reciprocal, nonreciprocal and adaptive categories. Early research on some of these characteristics has shown that this is a crucial category of influence (examples, Bachman *et al.* 1988b; Bachman *et al.* 1991).

Bachman's third category of influence is test taker personal characteristics or background characteristics. These include cultural background, background knowledge, cognitive abilities, sex and age. From the relatively few studies that have investigated these factors, it is clear that language tests should be sensitive to these factors in such a manner that test performance is not adversely influenced by these characteristics.

Bachman's (1990) fourth category that influences language test performance is random measurement error, which is made up of interactions among components of communicative language ability, test method facets, personal characteristics and measurement error.

Summing up, the nature and extent of influence of the factors of test methods, test taker characteristics and random factors should be understood well so as to minimize their influences on test performance so that the scores obtained on language tests reflect language ability and not other factors. Bachman (1990:156) puts forward this central idea best:

> The effects of both the test method and the interaction between test takers' individual characteristics and the methods used in language tests may reduce the effect on test performance of the language abilities we want to measure, and hence the interpretability of scores.

Thus, it seems clear that these four factors need to be examined when construct validation of test score use is contemplated.

Factors that influence second language acquisition (SLA)

Several attempts have been made in the last three decades to propose models that can explain the cognitive, cultural, educational, linguistic, psychological and social factors that influence SLA.

Three decades ago, Carroll's (1962) interactional model of school learning identified two major classes of variables: instructional and individual difference factors. The sub-categories of instructional factors are time and instructional excellence and the sub-categories of individual differences are general intelligence, aptitude, and motivation. This model can be seen as a precursor to present-day models which consider individual differences in SLA.

Naiman *et al.* (1978) proposed the "Good Language Learner" model though the model is only a listing of the classes of variables that affect SLA. The model proposes three independent variables: teaching, the learner and the context; and two dependent variables: learning and outcome. Schumann's (1978) acculturation model argues that "SLA is just one aspect of acculturation and the degree to which a learner acculturates to the target language group will control the degree to which he acquires the second language" (p. 34). Thus, acculturation is determined by the social and psychological distance between the learner and the target language.

Gardner's (1979, 1985) social-educational model of SLA, an intervening factors model, is concerned with the role of individual differences in SLA. Based on Lambert's social psychological model and the Carroll (1962) model, the Gardner model presents schematically four classes of variables: social milieu, individual differences, SLA contexts and outcome. Social milieu is identified as the cultural beliefs in the community, individual differences is further classified into intelligence, language aptitude, motivation, and situational anxiety, SLA contexts into formal language training and informal language experience, and outcome into linguistic and non-linguistic. Several other models like the Giles and Byrne (1982) intergroup model, Clement's (1980) and Clement and Kruidenier's (1985) social context model, and the Harley *et al.* (1987) and the Cummins and Swain (1986) studies, have addressed similar concerns.

Dulay *et al.* (1982) proposed a linear model:

$$\text{Input} \rightarrow \begin{array}{c} \textbf{Affective} \\ \textbf{filter} \end{array} \rightarrow \begin{array}{c} \textbf{Cognitive} \\ \textbf{organizers} \end{array} \rightarrow \textbf{Monitor} \rightarrow \textbf{Output}$$

This model proposed that three factors affect the output: the affective filter, the cognitive organizers, and the monitor. Krashen (1985) linked this model to five hypotheses: the acquisition-learning hypothesis, the natural sequence hypothesis, the monitor hypothesis, the affective filter hypothesis, and the comprehensible input hypothesis.

In terms of individual differences, three areas of variation can be seen:

1 **the monitor users**, where 'over-users' are those, in the words of Skehan (1989), "whose constant striving for correctness inhibits output" and 'under-users' "whose lack of concern with correctness leads to garrulous but less grammatical performance" (p.2-3);

2 **the affective filter**, which refers to the learner's openness or lack of anxiety; and

3 **the quantity of comprehensible input**, which is determined by the environment, in most cases a school of some kind. The quantity of comprehensible input can also be characterized as previous exposure to the target language in an acquisition type setting, for example, in a country where English is used widely.

While these brief descriptions of models in SLA are not exhaustive, they provide an introduction to one aspect of this study, namely, the investigation of relationships among the different test taker characteristics. As the brief descriptions have shown, several factors may affect SLA: instructional factors (Carroll 1962) and individual difference factors like cultural (Gardner 1979, 1985), affective

(Schumann 1978; Krashen 1985), cognitive (Naiman *et al.* 1978; Krashen 1985) and socio-educational (Gardner 1979, 1985). Not all of these factors or variables, however, have been empirically tested, as some of them are not easily operationalizable (for example, Krashen's acquisition-learning or comprehensible input hypotheses), while others present difficulties for data collection (for example, Carroll's intelligence and aptitude), as measures for intelligence and aptitude may not be easily available in the native languages of all subjects.

In summary, Bachman's (1990) general model for explaining performance on language tests as well as Gardner's (1979, 1985) socio-educational model of SLA provide useful frameworks to investigate the influence of cultural, educational, cognitive and social factors on language performance. In addition, Krashen's monitor hypothesis and the exposure factor are specific variables that will be investigated in this study.

Empirical studies

Nature of second language proficiency

Many language testing researchers have empirically investigated the nature of second language proficiency in the last two decades. Studies typically took the form of analyses of the internal structure of tests in order to find support or find arguments against Oller's (1976, 1979) unitary trait hypothesis. Some examples of such studies were: Oller and Hinofotis (1980), Hisama (1980), Hendricks *et al.* (1980) and Scholz *et al.* (1980).

Briefly, Oller's (1983) "Evidence for a general language proficiency factor: An expectancy grammar" summed up the argument for a unitary trait hypothesis which stated that language proficiency consists of a single, global ability, which he called "a pragmatic expectancy grammar". The evidence for this claim came from factor analytic studies on a wide range of language tests that loaded most heavily on a single factor which then came to be called a "g-factor", meaning a general language proficiency factor. Subsequent studies conducted on similar as well as new data showed that Oller's unitary trait hypothesis was untenable (Bachman and Palmer 1981; Upshur and Homburg 1983) and that his studies were methodologically flawed (Carroll 1983; Vollmer and Sang 1983). Oller then withdrew his claim and stated later in 1983 that "the unitary trait hypothesis was wrong" (p.352).

From then on, language testing researchers have found time and again that language proficiency consists of several distinct abilities that are either related to each other or that are related to a general higher order ability; for example, Carroll (1983), Bachman (1982), Bachman and Palmer (1982, 1983), Bachman *et al.* (1990), Davidson (1988), Kunnan (1992) and Sang *et al.* (1986). And, using large samples from TOEFL administrations, Swinton and Powers (1980),

Dunbar (1982), and Hale *et al.* (1989) found that the factor structure of the TOEFL is multi-componential. Furthermore, other studies conducted on different components of language ability again confirmed the multi-componential view of language proficiency; for example, speaking and reading (Bachman and Palmer 1981), oral communication (Hinofotis 1983), pronunciation (Purcell 1983), FSI oral interview (Bachman and Palmer 1983), cloze (Turner 1989) and listening and reading (Buck 1989).

In a more recent study, Fouly *et al.* (1990) investigated the nature of second language proficiency with respect to its divisibility and components. Two specific hypotheses, a correlated three-traits model and a higher/second-order with three traits model, were evaluated using a wide range of proficiency measures. The results of the study provided evidence to support both models. Thus, though studies have indicated that the nature of second language proficiency is not unitary, research has not unambiguously shown that there are a certain number of components, both higher/second order and primary factors, and what these consist of.

Factors that influence language test performance

Though the nature of second language proficiency has been a central concern among language testing researchers, not much research has focused on the factors that influence test performance. Several kinds of factors are argued by different researchers as causing differential test performance. Bachman (1990) argues that communicative language ability, test method and test taker characteristics are three important categories of influence apart from random factors. While the influence of (communicative) language ability on test performance is quite obvious, the influence of test method has been shown to be an important influence in several studies (Clifford 1978; Bachman *et al.*1995; Bachman and Palmer 1981, 1982, 1989; Oller 1972; Shohamy 1983, 1984). This influence will not be discussed further as it is not examined in this study.

In Bachman's (1990) characterization of the third category of influence, test taker characteristics consist of cultural background, background knowledge, cognitive abilities, sex and age. Gardner and Clement (1990), from the SLA literature, classify **individual difference variables** as
1 **cognitive characteristics**,
2 **attitudes and motivation**, and
3 **personality attributes and the sociostructural perspective** (or the linguistic, cognitive, and developmental context) of a particular language.
These two lists overlap but are not entirely similar as they come from different perspectives.

A discussion of the characteristics relevant to this study, namely, cultural background, exposure to the target language, motivation and monitoring follows.

Cultural background

Cultural background is used here broadly to include linguistic (native language), cultural (ethnicity) and educational factors. Early work in language testing showed a concern for culture-fair tests when tests were developed for monolingual/cultural groups; well-known examples are the work of Briere (1968, 1973) and Briere and Brown (1971) in developing tests for use with Native Indians. More recent work has been in the area of understanding how test performances of multi-cultural groups are affected by tests: the work of Farhady (1979) is a good example. He argued that there is a significant difference in the performance of foreign students who are from different language and educational backgrounds (in this case, students from Israel and Taiwan) in how they score on discrete-point and integrative tests.

Other examples include Vernon *et al.* (1986) and Welch *et al.* (1989) who have investigated the cultural influences on patterns of abilities in North America and differential performance in writing for black and white college freshman respectively. Test bias or differential item functioning literature (Berk 1982; Holland and Wainer 1993) abounds with studies that have investigated the effect of culture and native language on test performance; a few studies that are relevant to EFL are Chen and Henning (1985), Kunnan (1990), Oltman *et al.* (1988), and Zeidner (1986, 1987). In addition, Laosa (1991) has convincingly argued that population generalizability "is indeed a pivotal dimension of construct validity" (p.6), therefore exhorting researchers to "establish generalizability boundaries that accurately demarcate the populations to which the accumulated empirical data permit generalizing" (p.6).

Exposure

Exposure to the target language is obviously critical for SLA. But exposure can come in different ways and the influences of these different ways on SLA as well as test performance has not been investigated widely. For example, students of a second or foreign language can be exposed to the target language through a formal school setting in their home country, through an informal situation in their home country or through a formal school setting or informal situation in a country where English is used as a first language. To confound this situation further, some students may have a combination of these different situations in their learning history. Thus, exposure is difficult to capture, and no study has used this information to investigate the effect of exposure on test performance.

Krashen's (1985) "input hypothesis" is a related concept to exposure though this hypothesis is presented within his acquisition-learning distinction. **Acquisition**, according to Krashen is similar to the ways children develop first language competence; a subconscious process, and results in implicit knowledge of the language while **learning** is knowing about language or formal knowledge of language. Empirical research from caretaker speech in first language acquisition in children (Cross 1977; Newport *et al*. 1977), and some ambiguous support from SLA researchers (for example, Freed 1980; Gaies 1977) is the only evidence in support of the input hypothesis.

Attitude and motivation

Two early studies (Jones 1941, 1950) reported significant though low correlations between attitudes toward learning a language and second language proficiency. Gardner and Lambert (1959) reported that achievement in French as a second language loaded on two independent factors: social motivation and language aptitude. Considerable research has since been conducted in different language settings reported in Gardner (1985), Gardner and Lambert (1972), and Gardner and Lysynchuk (in press). Generally, from the research reported, it seems that indices of motivation correlate more highly with proficiency than do indices of attitudes (Gardner *et al*. 1976). Lambert (1963, 1967) demonstrated that attitudes and motivation were both cause and effect of successful second language achievement.

Research by Murakami (1980) and Oller *et al*. (1980) indicates that low to moderate correlations exist between these concepts and second language achievement, while Johnson and Krug (1980), investigating similar notions, found conflicting results. A number of full blown models based on these concepts, though emphasizing different processes, were then developed and tested: Clement's (1980) social context model, Gardner's (1985, 1988) socio-educational model and Giles and Byrne's (1982) intergroup model. In addition, Fouly (1985), Wang (1988), Ecob (1987), and Bachman and Mack (1986) presented models that included motivation, learning difficulties, social class and socio-economic status of the subjects in their studies.

Monitoring

Krashen's (1985) monitor hypothesis forms the basis for this characteristic among second language learners. His hypothesis is that second language learners monitor their performance when three conditions are met. The performer must:

1 have enough time. (In normal conversation, there is rarely enough time to consult conscious rules);
2 focus on form; and
3 know the rule. Krashen goes on to say that all these three conditions are met when students are given discrete-point grammar tests.

Empirical research that supports the notion of monitoring comes from Naiman *et al*. (1978) who uncovered a large number of specific techniques of monitoring and Rubin (1981) who reported the use of two aspects of monitoring:

1 correcting error in own/other's pronunciation, vocabulary, spelling, grammar, style etc., and
2 noting sources of own errors. The O'Malley *et al*. (1985) research on strategy finds monitoring to be only one of the many metacognitive strategies.

Structural modeling

Structural modeling or structural equation modeling or linear structural equation modeling is an *ex post facto* correlational approach that provides the mechanism for an investigation of relationships in the confirmatory factor analysis mode. Specifically, as Bentler (1989) puts it, "linear structural equation modeling is a useful methodology for statistically specifying, estimating, and testing hypothesized relationships among a set of substantively meaningful variables" (p.ix). Structural modeling can be best thought of as a coming together of two approaches to model fitting: multiple regression and factor analysis. As Ecob and Cuttance (1987:9) put it

> *the multiple regression approach expresses the relationship of a dependent variable to a number of regressor variables ... in contrast, the factor analysis approach finds a number of underlying or latent variables (or factors) that account for the common relationship among a number of observed variables.*

Briefly, the regression model specifies a directional relationship between two sets of variables, the dependent variable and a set of regressor variables. This system of equations is also known as path analysis. In the factor analysis model, relationships among the observed variables are explained in terms of the relation of each observed variable to a number of latent or unobserved variables or constructs and in terms of the relations of the latent constructs to one another. The structural equation model is the integration of both these models, providing the mechanism to hypothesize relationships among unobserved latent factors or constructs. This is what makes structural equation modeling more appealing than exploratory factor analysis and the multitrait–multimethod approach, both of which are popular among language testing researchers. A discussion of how structural models are specified is presented in Chapter 3.

The usefulness of structural modeling has been highlighted by many researchers (for example, Bentler 1978, 1986; Bollen and Long 1993; Kunnan 1994; Muthen 1988, 1989a). Recent studies and dissertations that have used structural modeling include those by Clement and Kruidenier (1985), Delandshere (1986), Ecob (1987), Gardner *et al.* (1983, 1987), Hill (1987), Nelson *et al.* (1984), Fouly (1985), Sasaki (1991) and Wang (1988).

Well-known software that has implemented linear structural equations include LISREL (Linear Structural Relations) developed by Joreskog and Sorbom (1984), EQS developed by Bentler (1989) and LISCOMP developed by Muthen (1987). The illustration that follows reports a "causal model" (Gardner *et al.* 1987) using LISREL.

An illustrative modeling study

This illustrative modeling study is by Gardner *et al.* (1987). They investigated the nature of French as a second language skills "lost by grade 12 students over the course of the summer vacation, and the role played by attitudes and motivation in promoting language achievement and language maintenance" (p. 29). The focus of this study is on the hypothesized relationships among language attitudes, motivation, use, and language retention or attrition, with motivation as an intervening factor. This model uses structural equation modeling with the LISREL software (Joreskog and Sorbom 1984). The model is presented in Figure 2.1.

Preliminaries

Paraphrasing Bachman (1988), in this model, the observed variables, AFC, INT, IFL, FTE, FCO, ALF, MI, US1, US2, ... LC are represented by square boxes. Associated with each of these observed variables is a "unique" component, or factor, represented by the greek letters **delta** and **epsilon**. The latent or unobserved variables, Language Attitudes (LAT), Motivation (MOT), Use (US), Achievement 1 (ACH1), and Achievement 2 (ACH2) are represented by circles. The first three unobserved variables are independent variables and the last two are dependent variables. Straight, single-headed lines with arrows indicate paths of direct relationships, for example,

LAT → MOT or ACH1 → ACH2

Double-headed lines represent correlations with no causation, for example, LC and LC or SR and SR. The numbers associated with the paths are estimates of parameters or path coefficients which indicate the strength of the relationships. These values could theoretically range from +1.00 to -1.00.

Results

The results of this study show that in general the observed variables load heavily on the unobserved hypothesized variables, indicating that the former are good measures of the latter. The indices of the goodness of fit of this model to the data are adequate: the model resulted in a χ^2 of 113.73 with 105 degrees of freedom. This statistic suggests that there is a good fit between the data and the model. Other indices of fit that are reported are: the ratio of χ^2 to degrees of freedom which is only 1.08 and compares favorably with the ratio of 5.0 suggested by Wheaton *et al.* (1977); the goodness of fit index of 0.882; an adjusted goodness of fit of 0.828 and the root mean square residual of 0.063. All these indices indicate that the model adequately describes the correlations obtained among the measures, or to say it more simply, there is a good fit of the model to the data.

Criticisms

Though this model is quite clearly represented and it fits the data well, there are some problems with it. For example, the values for the uniqueness components associated with the observed variables (the ones in the square boxes) are not

Figure 2.1

Gardner's causal model linking attitudes and motivation to language achievement, use and retention

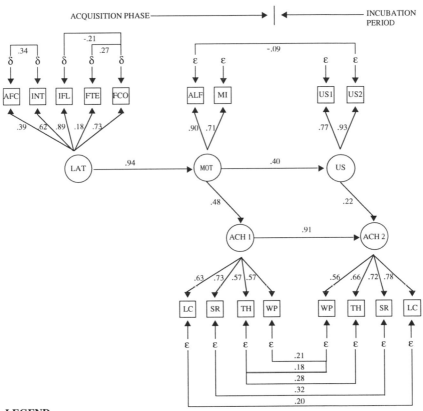

LEGEND

LAT   Language attitudes

AFC   Attitudes toward French Canadians
INT   Degree of integrativeness
IFL   Interest in foreign languages
FTE   Evaluation of the French instructor
FCO   Evaluation of the French course

MOT   Motivation

ALF   Attitudes toward learning French
MI   Motivational intensity

ACH 1   Achievement 1

LC   Listening comprehension
SR   Self-ratings (Can-do)

TH   Theme test
WP   Word production
δ, ε   Errors of measurement

US   Use

US1   Use of French phase 1
US2   Use of French phase 2

ACH 2   Achievement 2

WP   Word production
TH   Theme test
SR   Self-ratings (Can-do)
LC   Listening comprehension

shown. This is a drawback of the reporting as these values could have determined what the problems were with some of these variables. For example, the observed variable FTE, which belongs to the unobserved construct, LAT, has a loading of only 0.18 but the associated error value is not shown. It would have been helpful to have these in order to assess the relative influence of these errors on the particular measure.

Bachman (1988:201-2) criticizes this model and study on two counts: first, on the use of test methods as measures of proficiency:

> *In this study ... Gardner* et al. *used ten different indicators of language proficiency, but grouped these together more or less according to the test method used, rather than by the language abilities measured. The self-ratings, for example, included indicators of speaking, understanding, reading and writing, but these were aggregated into a single indicator, "SR". And although the factor loadings indicate that the measures included in the model are all reasonably good indicators of some "general" L2 achievement, treating indicators of different abilities as if they were all measuring the same ability ignores, it seems to me, recent LT research.*

Bachman's second argument is even more important for SLA researchers who use language tests:

> *... a second weakness, in my opinion, is in the measures of language achievement ... much current thinking in applied linguistics views language proficiency as consisting of competencies in both the formal ... and the functional or pragmatic aspects of language, a view that is generally supported in language testing ... there is a growing corpus of language tests that attempt to operationalize this broadened view of language ability. One would, therefore, reasonably expect SLA researchers to begin utilizing as criteria for their studies language tests that are based on more current views of language proficiency and more in keeping with current practice in the measurement of communicative competence.*

In addition to these criticisms, there are three other problems:
1 correlated errors, for example, between TH and WP or IFL and FCO appear to have no substantive justification;
2 neither the R^2 statistic nor the factor disturbances (or residuals) are reported; and
3 the study does not indicate whether the final model reported was the first or the only one tested in the study and whether model specification was used to arrive at this model.

Summary

To sum up, the above review of the literature of theoretical models, empirical studies of factors that influence language test performance and language achievement as well as the illustrative model show that research in this area is valuable for the fields of language testing and SLA, and that more research needs to be done. The review also clearly shows that though considerable research has been done, the strengths and directions of the relationships between test taker characteristics and language test performance have not been definitively established. For example, it is not clearly known which test taker characteristics are salient and not salient in different settings.

This is probably due to several factors. First, researchers are conducting and reporting on research from diverse perspectives, settings and countries. This does not make for clear translations for all situations. Second, the goals and purposes of researchers are diverse as some are exploring relationships, some confirming or disconfirming theories or hypotheses, some use correlation, others use exploratory factor analyses, and yet others use confirmatory factor analysis techniques. Third, researchers have different designs: some are experimental, some are non-experimental, and yet others are descriptive. Fourth, researchers use tools, instruments and measures (questionnaires, tests, interview or observation techniques) that are at one end of the scale standardized, and at the other end previously untested and home-made; both types could be valid, reliable, appropriate as well as highly invalid, unreliable and inappropriate. And, finally, all researchers do not use rigorous methodological techniques. For example, Dulay and Burt (1978) report that they rejected 95% of the studies they surveyed for failure to meet methodological standards, while Freedman (1987), Bachman (1988), Fouly (1985) and Wang (1988) criticize use of inappropriate measures, misapplication of model/analysis mismatch, and violations of statistical assumptions.

3 The structural modeling approach and its application to this study

Overview

The approach used in this study is structural modeling. As outlined in the previous section, it is a methodology for specifying, estimating and testing hypothesized relationships among variables. The statistical software program EQS (Bentler 1989) which is available at the University of California, Los Angeles (UCLA) on the mainframe system is used for this purpose.

Though the most popular approach in structural modeling is confirmatory in mode, this study is an exploratory one. This is in keeping with the philosophical position of this study which is to explore the relationships among variables. In addition, many of the variables in this study are being investigated for the first time using such a methodology, and there is not enough substantive research to form a complete theory for all the variables which could be tested. If a model that is posited in this study fits the data, and a clear theory emerges from the model fit, another data set can be used for confirmation of the structural relationships found in this study.

Data

Subjects

Data for this study were collected as part of the data for the Cambridge-TOEFL comparability study (CTCS) conducted at the University of Illinois at Urbana-Champaign, the University of Cambridge, and the University of California, Los Angeles (Bachman *et al.* 1995). Data from a total of 1,448 subjects from eight sites in eight countries were used in this study. The sites and sample sizes were: Bangkok (Thailand), 169; Cairo (Egypt), 89; Osaka (Japan), 189; Hong Kong (Hong Kong), 196; Madrid (Spain), 196; Sao Paulo (Brazil), 207; Toulouse (France), 197; and Zurich (Switzerland), 205.

Descriptive information collected from all the subjects (n= 1448) through the background questionnaire was as follows: the majority of the subjects (also referred to this study as test takers) were enrolled either as students, at the secondary school level (21.3%), or at the college level (full time, 27.6% ; part time, 10.45%) or in a language institute or other English course (17%), while

23.1% were not enrolled as students. The median age was 21, with the youngest test taker 14 years of age and the eldest 58, and slightly over half (59.4%) were female. Preparation for the TOEFL and FCE tests differed in the sample: while 90.4% of the sample had not taken a preparation course for the TOEFL, 50.5% had taken a preparation course for the FCE. Table 3.1 presents descriptive information on educational status and Table 3.2 presents test preparation, both by site. These tables are summarized from Table 14 in Bachman *et al.* (1995).

Table 3.1

Educational status by site in percentages

Site	SS	PTC	FTC	LI	NA
Thailand	3.5	5.3	32.7	4.1	54.4
Egypt	3.5	3.5	19.8	24.4	48.8
Japan	0.0	0.8	86.4	3.2	9.6
Hong Kong	86.5	1.1	5.6	2.9	3.4
Spain	15.8	9.3	53.0	13.7	8.2
Brazil	26.0	41.2	9.8	10.8	12.3
Switzerland	0.0	2.0	4.9	54.1	39.0

Notes: SS=Secondary school; PTC=Part-time college; FTC= Full-time college; LI=Language institute; NA=Not enrolled; information from France was not available due to a clerical error in administering the background questionnaire.

Table 3.2

Test preparation by site in percentages

Site	TOEFL Yes	FCE Yes
Thailand	30.4	8.8
Egypt	17.0	62.1
Japan	18.4	0.8
Hong Kong	1.7	7.3
Spain	2.6	78.9
Brazil	3.9	97.1
Switzerland	3.0	75.0

Instruments

The instruments used for this study were a background questionnaire consisting of 45 Likert scaled items which collected test taker characteristics information; and a group of EFL tests from the University of Cambridge Local Examinations Syndicate (UCLES), United Kingdom, and the Educational Testing Service (ETS), Princeton, New Jersey.

Background questionnaire/test taker characteristics

The background questionnaire (also referred to in this study as test taker characteristics) was modified from a University of Illinois, Urbana-Champaign, questionnaire that was given to its entering foreign students. It was translated into the native languages of the subjects, and was administered to all the subjects either before the tests, during parts of the tests, or after the tests.

The questionnaire asked for responses from test takers regarding their current educational status (item 1) and whether they had taken a course to prepare for the TOEFL (item 2), the FCE (item 3) and the CPE (item 4, which will not be discussed in this study); their age (item 5); whether they had instruction in a formal (school) (items 6 to 13) or in an informal setting in their home country (items 14 to 18) or in a country where English is used as a first language, if they had visited one (items 19 to 29); their motivation to study English (items 30 to 37); and their frequency self monitoring English (items 38 to 45). These items are labelled as BQ 01 to BQ 45 for the analyses.

EFL tests

The EFL tests used for this study were: the **First Certificate in English** (FCE), developed and administered by UCLES, the **Test of English as a Foreign Language** (TOEFL), developed and administered by the Educational Testing Service, (ETS), the **Test of English Writing** (TEW), developed for the CTCS project, and the **Speaking Proficiency in English Assessment Kit** (SPEAK), a retired form of the **Test of Spoken English** (TSE) developed and administered by ETS. The details of the tests paper by paper are as follows:

1 **FCE Paper 1** (FCE1) is entitled "Reading Comprehension", and includes two sections, items 1 through 25, which test language usage or language use, and items 26 through 40 which are based on reading passages. All items follow a four-option multiple-choice format;

2 **FCE Paper 2** (FCE2) is entitled "Composition", and consists of five prompts, from which the test taker chooses two. The test taker is expected to write 120 to 180 words in response to each prompt;

3 **FCE Paper 3** (FCE3) is entitled "Use of English" and includes items that test various aspects of lexicon, register and other elements of English usage. The items follow a variety of formats, ranging from gap-filling to short completion paragraph writing;

4 **FCE Paper 4** (FCE4) is entitled "Listening Comprehension" and is a tape-plus-booklet test. The items are passage-based, with test takers listening to a passage and then responding to several items on that passage. The test consists of several parts, each following a different format: they range from a variety of visual prompts with single sentences or charts, to diagrams and pictures;

5 **FCE Paper 5** (FCE5) is a face-to-face oral interview. The number of test takers and interviewers (or examiners) may vary from a ratio of one on one to one on two situations. The interview too may vary from one "information package" to another: the prompt material contains short reading passages, photographs or charts, and the topics include areas such as holidays, sports, or food and drink etc;

6 the **Test of English as a Foreign Language** (TOEFL) used for this study was an institutional form of the TOEFL which consisted of a form of the official international TOEFL that has been retired from operational use. There are three sections to the test:
Section 1 "Listening Comprehension" (TOEFL1),
Section 2 "Structure and Written Expression" (TOEFL2), and
Section 3 "Vocabulary and Reading Comprehension" (TOEFL3).
Item types vary somewhat but all follow a four-option multiple-choice format;

7 the **Test of English Writing** (TEW) which followed the format and scoring of the Test of Written English (TWE) developed by ETS, contains a single prompt which requires writing for up to 30 minutes;

8 the **Speaking Proficiency in English Assessment Kit** (SPEAK) is a semi-direct test of oral performance, and is the institutional version of the Test of Spoken English, developed by ETS. The SPEAK does not involve a face-to-face interaction but requires the test taker to respond to a tape recording which provides the prompts for the speaking. The test takers' responses are recorded on cassette tape. Table 3.11 (on page 47) presents names, labels and descriptions of variables and constructs.

Data collection and scoring procedures

All subjects recorded their responses to the 45 point background questionnaire on optical scan sheets that were then scanned. Their responses to the tests varied from test to test: FCE Papers 2, 3 and 4 and the TEW required writing in the responses, FCE Paper 5 required face-to-face oral responses, FCE paper 1 and the TOEFL required marking them on the optical scan sheets, and the SPEAK required responses to be spoken into a tape recorder.

The scoring procedures used for the tests followed the guidelines set by the respective test developers: the FCE Papers were scored based on marking schemes developed at UCLES, the TOEFL and SPEAK followed existing ETS procedures, and the TEW followed standard scoring procedures used for the TWE. But even among the UCLES Papers there were differences in scoring procedures: Paper 1 (reading comprehension) used an optically scanned multiple-choice sheet, Paper 2 (composition) and 3 (use) were subjectively marked by examiners, Paper 4 (listening comprehension) was scored against a key by clerical assistants, and Paper 5 (oral interview) was marked by the oral examiners. Among the other tests, the open-ended responses were scored in two different ways: the TEW was rated on a holistic scale of writing proficiency ranging from 1 to 6 but the SPEAK was scored using analytical procedures.

The study used separate subtest scores for each of the FCE and TOEFL papers or sections, a single composite score for the TEW, and four scores for the SPEAK: Grammar (SPK GRAM), Pronunciation (SPK PRON), Fluency (SPK FLCY) and Overall Comprehensibility (SPK COMP).

Data preparation

Data preparation for this study involved merging the two work data sets: the background questionnaire data set and the test data set. These two data sets were matched and merged by test taker identification number and site number. When the data sets were matched and merged, it was discovered that not all the subjects who had data from the questionnaire had test data and vice versa. The new combined data set had complete data for only 985 subjects; the other subjects, therefore, had to be deleted from the data set and the study. The new combined data set had item-level data for the background questionnaire items and subtest-level data for the tests for all subjects.

Structural modeling

Structural modeling or structural equation modeling, as outlined in Chapter 1, is a way of representing hypothesized relationships between constructs and observed variables and among constructs based on substantive theory and previous empirical research.

Statistical software: EQS

The statistical software used for the structural modeling in this study was EQS 3.0 version (Bentler 1989) which is limited to mean and covariance structure models. EQS implements a general mathematical and statistical approach to the analysis of linear structural equations systems. The EQS mathematical model subsumes several covariance and mean structural models which include multiple regression, path analysis and simultaneous equations, and the EQS statistical theory allows "for the estimation of parameters and testing of models using traditional multivariate normal theory" (Bentler 1989:1).

Other well-known statistical software that is used for structural modeling include LISREL (Joreskog and Sorbom 1984) and LISCOMP (Muthen 1987). Several studies in SLA and language testing research in recent years have used LISREL (Bachman and Palmer 1981, 1982; Clement and Kruidenier, 1985; Gardner 1985).

Model specification

Model specification in EQS is easy and straightforward: the observed or measured variables in the input data file are called variables or **Vs**; hypothetical or unmeasured latent variables are called factors or **Fs**; residual variation in measured variables is called errors or **Es**; and their corresponding residuals in factors are called disturbances or **Ds**. Other conventions that EQS uses are: measured variables are shown in squares; unmeasured variables are shown in circles; and all paths, in the form of unidirectional arrows, are drawn from the variables or factors hypothesized to be ones that can influence the variables or factors which are hypothesized to be ones that can be influenced. Curved two-headed paths between independent factors indicate correlation between them.

Specifying paths and writing equations

Paths between factors (Fs) were determined on the basis of the four research questions. The unidirectional arrows in both models indicate the hypothesized direction of the influence of some factors hypothesized to influence other factors. These relationships were then written in the form of equations so that EQS could translate them for the analysis of data in order to arrive at estimates for the variables and the constructs. An asterisk after a numerical value (for example, 1*F1) specifies that the parameter is to be estimated, with the numerical value (1) as a starting value. Here are examples of how some of the variables, factors, errors and disturbances in Model 1 were represented in equations (without start values):

$$
\begin{aligned}
V1 &= {}^*F1 + E1 \\
V2 &= {}^*F1 + E2 \\
V3 &= {}^*F1 + E3 \\
V4 &= {}^*F2 + E4 \\
V5 &= {}^*F2 + E5 \\
V6 &= {}^*F2 + E6 \\
V7 &= {}^*F3 + E7 \\
&\quad \vdots \\
V25 &= {}^*F5 + E25 \\
F5 &= {}^*F1 + {}^*F2 + {}^*F3 + {}^*F4 + D5 \\
F6 &= {}^*F1 + {}^*F2 + {}^*F3 + {}^*F4 + D6 \\
F7 &= {}^*F1 + {}^*F2 + {}^*F3 + {}^*F4 + D7 \\
F8 &= {}^*F1 + {}^*F2 + {}^*F3 + {}^*F4 + D8
\end{aligned}
$$

In addition, variances and covariances between factors, errors and disturbances were represented in the equations as well. These too were written with an asterisk after a numerical value so that these parameters could be estimated.

Estimation method

The specific estimation method used for the study was maximum likelihood as well as maximum likelihood with ROBUST. Maximum likelihood is used when the "normal theory" assumption that variables are multivariate normally distributed is met. But, as shown in Table 3.9, since the kurtosis and skewness of the variables for both the non Indo-European and the Indo-European groups were not perfectly normally distributed, it was considered safer to use maximum likelihood with ROBUST. ROBUST provides robust statistics like the Satorra-Bentler scaled test statistic that is designed to have a distribution that is more closely approximated by χ^2 than the usual statistic and robust standard errors that are correct in large samples even if the distributional assumptions about the variables are incorrect. Research has shown that robust statistics are more trustworthy than ordinary statistics (Chou *et al.* 1989).

Assessment of fit and the evaluation of models

As Cuttance (1987) states, the phrase assessment or "test of fit" of a model "refers to parametric statistical tests ... those based on a particular statistical distribution", and the phrase "evaluation of the model" "refers to measures of the methodological validity of a model" (p. 256).

The parametric tests of the assessment fit of models used in this study were:

1 **the χ^2 statistic** (also known as the likelihood ratio test) for the specified model against the unconstrained or null model. The smaller this statistic the better the model fit. However, since this statistic has been shown to be an acceptable test statistic only in the case of large samples and questioned in the case of small samples (Saris *et al.* 1987), Joreskog and Sorbom (1984) suggest that this statistic should be treated only as a heuristic index of goodness-of-fit rather than as a test statistic;

2 **the χ^2/df ratio** which was suggested by Wheaton *et al.* (1977) as a way of dealing with the effect of large sample size on the χ^2 statistic. Based on their experience, they suggested that a ratio of around 5.0 was reasonable for a sample size of about 1,000. In recent studies, however, many researchers have argued for a more conservative ratio: Stage (1990) has argued that 2.5 or less is a good fit of the model to the data;

3 **the Bentler-Bonett normed fit index (BBNFI) and the Bentler-Bonett nonnormed fit index (BBNNFI):** these indices developed by Bentler and Bonett (1980) are based on the fit function used as well as on the baseline model of uncorrelated or independent variables. In both cases the higher the

index, the better the model fit, though in the case of the Bentler-Bonett normed fit index the range is 0-1 and for the Bentler-Bonett nonnormed fit index the range could be out of 0-1. Although no rules of thumb have been clearly established, structural modelers seem to suggest that models with BBNFI and BBNNFI values of less than .80 are inadequate and that most acceptable models would have BBNFI and BBNNFI values of more than .90. In support of the BBNNFI, Wheaton (1987) states that it has the major advantage of reflecting model fit very well at all sample sizes. Both these indices are generally used as adjuncts to the χ^2 statistic;

4 **the Comparative Fit Index (CFI):** this index developed by Bentler (1990) avoids the underestimation of fit sometimes noted for the BBNFI in small samples. Bentler argues that the CFI is the preferred index. Once again, just as in the case of BBNFI and BBNNFI, models with .90 and higher are considered acceptable;

5 **the Satorra and Bentler scaled test statistic** developed by Satorra and Bentler (1988a, 1988b) that is computed as part of the robust statistics.

Following Cuttance (1987), the methods for assessing the methodological validity of models used in this study were:

1 an inspection of the parameter estimates to ascertain whether estimated correlations are in the 0-1 range and whether estimated variances of constructs, errors and disturbances as well as estimates of squared multiple correlations for all observed variables are all positive;

2 an inspection of the estimates of construct loadings to determine whether they are sufficiently high (generally higher than .25) to justify the interpretation of the constructs as measuring underlying theoretical constructs;

3 an inspection of the t-test values to check whether the parameter estimates are significant;

4 an inspection of the standardized residual matrix and the average and the average off-diagonal absolute standardized residuals to determine whether they are small and evenly distributed among variables (generally .05 and below).

Refining models

Finally, two procedures in EQS that helped refine the models by evaluating the parameters that were being estimated were the Lagrange Multiplier Test (LMTest) and the Wald Test (WTest). The Lagrange Multiplier Test tests restrictions on fixed parameters, such as "missing" paths or covariances that are set to zero in the model (and non zero in the population) that would be better treated as free parameters and estimated later. It also tests restrictions on equality constraints that are not consistent with the data and would be better if released. Thus, the Lagrange Multiplier Test suggests additions to parameters with the help of univariate and multivariate χ^2 statistics.

The Wald Test evaluates sets of parameters and suggests that sets of parameters that are treated as free in the models could be simultaneously set to zero without significant degradation to model fit. Thus, the Wald Test suggests dropping parameters with the help of z-test values.

However, it must be stated that these tests were used in this study to refine the two models only as recommendations because often the recommendations did not have the support of substantive theory, and therefore, they were not followed blindly.

Preliminary analysis

Preliminary analyses were done on the background questionnaire data (the test taker characteristics that were collected from the background questionnaire) and the test performance data. By treating the data as a single population, single-group analysis was done as initial exploration of the data.

Single-group analysis

An examination of the responses revealed that some branching (and categorical items) on the background questionnaire were not understood clearly (items 6, 13, 18, 21, and 27). For example, item (or, question, as used in this example) 6 was:

6   *Have you ever studied English in school or in a language institute*
        in the country you consider to be your home?
               (A)   yes
               (B)   no
        IF YES, ANSWER QUESTIONS 7-13.
        IF NO, GO TO QUESTION 13 ON PAGE 3.

Many subjects did not understand these directions clearly. So, irrespective of the IF YES/NO direction, they went on to the very next item.

There were other problems with the questionnaire: some items overlapped with other items (items 8, 22, 29) and some others had very low response rates (items 11, 12, 16, 19, 24, 25, 31, 33, 34, 35, 37, 38, 42 to 45). All these items were dropped from further analyses. Thus, a total of 21 items from the 45 items were chosen for this study. Of these items 1 to 3 ask for information regarding current educational status and test preparation and item 5 relates to age. Information collected from these items was presented earlier in this chapter. Item 4 dealt with the Certificate of Proficiency in English (CPE) test which is not part of this study. Therefore, only a total of 16 items were considered for further analyses in this study. (The questionnaire is presented in full in Appendix 1.)

Distributions and reliabilities

First, data from all 985 subjects treated as a single group were analyzed. Table 3.3 presents summary descriptive statistics for the 16 test taker characteristics. These statistics indicate that the distributions of all the items were reasonably normal.

Table 3.3

Distributions for test taker characteristics

Variable	Mean	Std dev	Kurtosis	Skewness
BQ07	3.51	1.22	-1.05	-0.22
BQ09	1.87	0.85	0.77	0.91
BQ10	2.46	0.86	0.51	0.72
BQ14	1.40	0.89	5.21	2.39
BQ15	1.22	1.90	-0.70	1.05
BQ17	1.30	0.55	4.57	2.00
BQ20	0.47	0.57	-0.02	0.78
BQ23	0.98	1.82	0.27	1.44
BQ26	1.46	1.06	4.94	2.45
BQ28	1.38	0.61	3.57	1.69
BQ30	1.39	0.56	0.86	1.21
BQ32	1.58	0.67	0.70	0.95
BQ36	1.93	0.73	0.25	0.53
BQ39	2.57	0.72	-0.06	0.12
BQ40	2.40	0.72	-0.31	-0.04
BQ41	2.87	0.76	-0.07	-0.33

Table 3.4 presents internal consistency reliability estimates for these items which were grouped into five scales based on the content of the items. The five scales were:
1 Home Country Formal instruction (HCF),
2 Home Country Informal exposure (HCI),
3 English Speaking Country instruction or exposure (ESC),
4 Motivation (MOT), and
5 Monitoring (MON).
The reliability estimates are reasonably high with the exception of the MOT scale. The basis for these scales is explained in Chapter 2.

Table 3.5 presents summary descriptive statistics for the tests or paper scores. These distributions are based on all subjects (N=985), after the computer file with the tests was matched and merged with the background questionnaire computer file. Score distributions indicate that all the measures are reasonably normally distributed.

Internal consistency reliability estimates for all the tests and sections are presented in Table 3.6. These figures were estimates computed by Bachman *et al.* (1995) for all subjects in the Cambridge TOEFL Comparability Study. They are being reported here because item-level data were not readily available. Further, these estimates were considered to be close to the estimates that could have been computed with the item-level data because the means and standard deviations presented in Table 3.5 (for N = 985) are close to those reported in Bachman *et al.* (1995) for all subjects.

Bachman *et al.* report that consistency of the averaged ratings for the TEW and SPEAK were estimated using single-facet generalizability studies with raters as facets. No reliabilities could be estimated for FCE Paper 2 and 5 because these papers are not re-rated operationally, or for section scores (SPK GRAM, SPK PRON and SPK FLCY) on SPEAK.

Table 3.4

Reliability estimates for test taker characteristics

Item	Construct	alpha
BQ 07	HCF	
BQ 09	HCF	
BQ 10	HCF	0.70
BQ 14	HCI	
BQ 15	HCI	
BQ 17	HCI	0.73
BQ 20	ESC	
BQ 23	ESC	
BQ 26	ESC	
BQ 28	ESC	0.75
BQ 30	MOT	
BQ 32	MOT	
BQ 36	MOT	0.52
BQ 39	MON	
BQ 40	MON	
BQ 41	MON	0.68

Table 3.5

Distributions for all tests

Variable	Mean	Std dev	Kurtosis	Skewness
FCE1	26.40	4.62	0.08	-0.47
FCE2	24.93	5.30	-0.28	0.02
FCE3	25.45	5.16	0.33	-0.53
FCE4	14.00	2.90	0.08	-0.62
FCE5	27.57	5.37	-0.26	0.01
TOEFL1	50.47	6.17	-0.05	-0.11
TOEFL2	51.89	6.45	-0.17	-0.14
TOEFL3	52.39	5.91	0.23	-0.46
TEW	3.92	0.84	0.55	-0.05
SPK GRAM	2.01	0.51	0.84	0.01
SPK PRON	2.16	0.43	1.03	0.82
SPK FLCY	2.02	0.50	1.01	0.04
SPK COMP	203.34	38.12	-0.12	-0.06

Table 3.6

Reliability estimates for all tests

Test	alpha
FCE1	.79
FCE2	NA
FCE3	.85
FCE4	.62
FCE5	NA
TOEFL1	.89
TOEFL2	.83
TOEFL3	.87
TEW	.90
SPK GRAM	NA
SPK PRON	NA
SPK FLCY	NA
SPK COMP	.97

Exploratory factor analysis

Test taker characteristics

Exploratory factor analysis of the test taker characteristics collected through the background questionnaire was done as an initial exploration of the data. First, a matrix of product-moment correlations among the 16 variables from the background questionnaire was used to perform exploratory factor analyses. Standard procedures for determining the "best" factor model were followed. Initial principal axes were extracted with squared multiple correlations on the diagonal of the matrix. The eigenvalues from initial extractions were examined for relative magnitude and graphed in a scree plot. Principal axes were then extracted with the number of factors generally equal to one above and one below the number of factors indicated by the "elbow" of the scree plot. These extractions were then rotated to both orthogonal and oblique solutions. A final determination about the best number of factors to extract was made on the basis of simple structure, which are patterns of strong loadings for variables on one factor and near-zero loadings on other factors, and interpretability, which are groupings of measures of a given construct that load on a factor.

In brief, the exploratory factor analysis results suggested an uncorrelated five factor solution with factors and the variables matching the questionnaire type. The factors, the variables numbers, and the names of the factors were as follows:
Factor 1: Variables BQ 07, 09, 10 (Home country formal instruction);
Factor 2: Variables BQ 14, 15, 17 (Home country informal exposure);
Factor 3: Variables BQ 20, 23, 26, 28 (English speaking country instruction or exposure);

Factor 4: Variables BQ 30, 32, 36 (Motivation);
Factor 5: Variables BQ 39, 40, 41 (Monitoring).
    Table 3.7 presents summarized results.

Table 3.7

EFA results of the test taker characteristics

Variable	Communality	Eigenvalue	% of var	Cum% of var
BQ07	.318	2.906	18.2	18.2
BQ09	.322	2.252	14.1	32.3
BQ10	.406	1.973	12.3	44.6
BQ14	.423	1.801	11.3	55.8
BQ15	.577	1.335	8.3	64.2
BQ17	.645	.924	5.8	69.9
BQ20	.518	.757	4.7	74.7
BQ23	.646	.719	4.5	79.2
BQ26	.529	.638	4.0	83.2
BQ28	.446	.550	3.4	86.6
BQ30	.200	.465	2.9	89.5
BQ32	.230	.442	2.8	92.3
BQ36	.102	.423	2.6	94.9
BQ39	.145	.360	2.2	97.2
BQ40	.305	.229	1.4	98.6
BQ41	.330	.227	1.4	100.0

	ESC Factor 1	HCI Factor 2	HCF Factor 3	MOT Factor 4	MON Factor 5	h^2
BQ07	.031	.071	.613	.043	.162	.410
BQ09	.110	.023	.632	.026	.007	.413
BQ10	.115	.014	.797	.060	.092	.661
BQ14	.040	.662	.068	.029	.088	.453
BQ15	.054	.788	.135	.041	.027	.645
BQ17	.007	.940	.017	.023	.011	.884
BQ20	.717	.009	.042	.104	.071	.531
BQ23	.887	.045	.089	.018	.017	.797
BQ26	.669	.008	.113	.053	.025	.464
BQ28	.660	.138	.055	.051	.029	.461
BQ30	.054	.033	.021	.066	.579	.344
BQ32	.015	.036	.096	.053	.702	.507
BQ36	.087	.044	.066	.013	.295	.101
BQ39	.013	.045	.063	.425	.015	.187
BQ40	.018	.010	.004	.673	.059	.457
BQ41	.107	.042	.032	.763	.021	.597
Eigen value	2.486	1.938	1.463	1.261	.763	7.911
%of h^2	15.5	12.1	9.1	7.9	4.8	49.400

Note: ESC – English Speaking Country instruction or exposure; HCI – Home Country Informal exposure; HCF – Home Country Formal instruction; MOT – Motivation; MON – Monitoring.

EFL test performance

Results from the exploratory factor analysis of the EFL test performance done by Bachman *et al.* (1995) were used for this study. Bachman *et al.* report that the best solution was one with an orthogonalized general factor and four primary factors. The primary factors were:

Factor 1: FCE papers 1, 2, 3 – an FCE written mode factor;

Factor 2: TOEFL sections 2 and 3, and TEW – an ETS written mode;

Factor 3: FCE papers 4 and 5, and TOEFL section 1 – interactional listening and speaking; and

Factor 4: SPEAK – non-interactional listening and speaking.

Table 3.8, which is summarized from Bachman *et al.* (1995), presents the initial communalities and eigenvalues and the orthogonalized factor matrix with a second-order general factor solution.

Table 3.8

EFA results for all tests

Variable	Communality	Eigenvalue	% of var	Cum % of var
FCE1	.590	7.484	57.6	57.6
FCE2	.522	1.325	10.2	67.8
FCE3	.665	.653	5.0	72.8
FCE4	.480	.577	4.4	77.2
FCE5	.428	.553	4.3	81.5
TOEFL1	.599	.502	3.9	85.3
TOEFL2	.601	.388	3.0	88.3
TOEFL3	.619	.372	2.9	91.2
TEW	.396	.343	2.6	93.8
SPK GRAM	.805	.253	1.9	97.9
SPK PRON	.630	.200	1.5	99.4
SPK FLCY	.777	.073	0.6	100.0
SPK COMP	.896	.276	2.1	96.0

 $\Rightarrow$

Table 3.8 (continued)

	General factor	Factor 1	Factor 2	Factor 3	Factor 4	h^{2*}
FCE1	.754	-.031	.078	.175	.104	.617
FCE2	.711	.074	-.023	.270	.002	.584
FCE3	.820	-.026	.028	.341	-.004	.789
FCE4	.704	-.004	-.048	.053	.236	.556
FCE5	.621	.173	-.028	.015	.165	.443
TOEFL1	.776	.058	.059	-.043	.284	.692
TOEFL2	.680	.049	.573	-.004	.010	.793
TOEFL3	.711	-.085	.419	.032	.102	.699
TEW	.581	.074	.223	.097	.012	.402
SPK GRAM	.642	.621	.015	-.000	-.000	.798
SPK PRON	.707	.333	-.026	.131	.030	.630
SPK FLCY	.676	.555	-.021	.007	.045	.767
SPK COMP	.705	.719	.040	.011	-.034	1.018
Eigenvalue	6.401	1.377	.570	.252	.189	8.789
% variance	49.200	10.600	4.400	1.900	1.500	67.600

Orthogonalized factor matrix with second-order general factor

* Communality

Multiple-group analysis

Bachman *et al.* (1995) found significant differential performance from site to site on these EFL tests. Their analysis, which was based on a canonical discriminant analysis, indicated that there were considerable differences in test performance across sites, with subjects in three non Indo-European native language background groups performing the lowest on the tests of reading and writing, and subjects in two of these performing the lowest on the listening and speaking tests.

Thus, the sites of subjects with native languages which are from the non Indo-European language families seemed to be different from sites of subjects with native languages which are from the Indo-European language family. In addition, it was thought that these two groups not only had native languages that belonged to different language groups but they also differed in the status of English in their countries and in their educational systems. Laosa's (1991) exhortation which requires a multiple-group analysis for construct validation studies seemed to fit this case perfectly. For these reasons, multiple-group analyses became the focus of the present study. Subjects from Thailand (native language: Thai), Egypt (Arabic), Japan (Japanese), and Hong Kong (Chinese) were grouped together as the non Indo-European (NIE) group and Spain (Spanish), Brazil (Portuguese), France (French) and Switzerland (German) were grouped together as the Indo-European (IE) one. The NIE group had 380 subjects and the IE group had 605 subjects after all cases with missing data were dropped from the study.

Distributions and reliabilities

Table 3.9 presents distributions for the NIE and IE groups. The differences between the two groups on the background questionnaire items BQ 07 to BQ 41 were apparent as fourteen out of the sixteen items were significantly different (p < .001) in a one-way analysis of variance. The differential performance on the tests too was clear: the IE group had higher scores for all tests compared to the NIE group; also, on seven out of the ten tests (or seven out of thirteen scores as the SPEAK has four scores), there was a significant difference (p < .001) in a one-way analysis of variance between the two groups. In terms of individual variables, only one variable (BQ 26) seemed to violate normality with a kurtosis of 21.69 and skewness of 4.56 for the NIE group. Thus, it was decided to drop this variable from further analysis, reducing the test taker characteristics to fifteen.

Reliability estimates for the test taker characteristics for both groups are presented in Table 3.10. Reliability estimates were reasonably high for both groups except for the HCF construct group which was quite low for both groups and the MOT construct group which was low for the NIE group and lower still for the IE group.

This indicated that the MOT construct group items were not very reliable for these two groups. In addition, since MOT also had low reliabilities for the whole group and low communalities (from the EFA results), it was decided at this stage that the MOT construct group should be dropped from this study, further reducing the test taker characteristics to twelve.

Table 3.9

**Distributions for test taker characteristics and all tests for both groups;
NIE Group, N=380; IE group, N=605**

Variable	NIE Group				IE Group			
	Mean	Std dev	Kurt	Skew	Mean	Std dev	Kurt	Skew
BQ07	4.35	1.09	2.40	-1.80	2.99*	1.00	-.20	.28
BQ09	2.25	.97	-.32	.43	1.63*	.63	.68	.73
BQ10	3.15	.78	.08	.41	2.04*	.58	3.11	.76
BQ14	1.43	.96	4.52	2.32	1.38	.83	5.62	2.42
BQ15	.92	1.76	.52	1.52	1.41*	1.96	-1.14	.81
BQ17	1.27	.55	5.47	2.27	1.31	.54	4.12	1.84
BQ20	.35	.56	1.51	1.39	.54*	.56	-.45	.46
BQ23	.45	1.33	6.27	2.81	1.31*	1.99	-.87	.98
BQ26	1.14	.56	21.69	4.56	1.66*	1.23	2.20	1.87
BQ28	1.23	.56	10.73	2.99	1.48*	.61	1.56	1.15
BQ30	1.31	.53	2.31	1.60	1.44*	.58	.31	1.01
BQ32	1.44	.59	1.65	1.25	1.67*	.69	.37	.79
BQ36	1.82	.71	-.18	.49	2.00*	.73	.49	.57
BQ39	2.36	.70	.64	.48	2.70*	.71	-.10	-.07
BQ40	2.25	.73	-.42	.03	2.49*	.70	-.23	-.04
BQ41	2.76	.83	-.33	-.23	2.94*	.71	.07	-.34
FCE1	24.68	4.92	-.38	-.29	27.48*	4.06	.27	-.40
FCE2	23.20	5.55	-.62	.10	26.02*	4.83	-.16	.18
FCE3	23.37	5.75	-.36	-.28	26.76*	4.27	.45	-.30
FCE4	12.79	3.28	-.73	-.33	14.69*	2.41	.17	-.45
FCE5	25.99	5.72	-.37	.22	28.55*	4.90	-.12	.03
TOEFL1	49.11	6.23	.12	-.03	51.32	5.98	-.11	-.15
TOEFL2	50.42	6.56	-.32	.02	52.81	6.21	.06	-.21
TOEFL3	49.89	6.41	-.05	-.27	53.96*	4.97	-.27	-.21
TEW	3.65	.89	-.23	.07	4.10*	.77	1.45	.08
SPK GRAM	1.85	.44	-.38	.29	2.00	.42	-.08	.12
SPK PRON	2.00	.33	-.10	-.30	2.25	.30	1.01	-.63
SPK FLCY	1.85	.42	-.40	.13	2.04	.39	-.09	-.10
SPK COMP	194.40	38.79	-.41	.03	208.96	36.62	.14	-.07

* Significant differences between the two groups at $p < .001$

Table 3.10

Reliability estimates for test taker characteristics for both groups

Item	Construct	Non Indo-European group alpha	Indo-European group alpha
BQ07	Home country formal		
BQ09	Home country formal		
BQ10	Home country formal	0.53	0.53
BQ14	Home country informal		
BQ15	Home country informal		
BQ17	Home country informal	0.78	0.62
BQ20	English speaking country		
BQ23	English speaking country		
BQ28	English speaking country	0.78	0.73
BQ30	Motivation		
BQ32	Motivation		
BQ36	Motivation	0.55	0.45
BQ39	Monitoring		
BQ40	Monitoring		
BQ41	Monitoring	0.61	0.64

Summary

Based on these preliminary analyses, it was decided to investigate the relationships among the twelve test taker characteristics and the thirteen test performance variables for the two groups, the non Indo-European and the Indo-European groups, separately. This decision was made because there was fairly strong evidence from the differential performance in the tests to suggest that the two groups are from different population groups.

Further, this approach offered the possibility of formulating different specific research questions for each of the groups as well as structurally modeling the multiple-group data separately because on the basis of preliminary analysis it appeared unlikely that the hypotheses and models proposed would fit the single-group data. When such differences between groups exist, following Laosa (1991), construct validation studies like this one need to demarcate the (two) populations so that correct inferences are possible from the separate analyses.

Methodologically, since the purpose of this study was to explore the relationships among these variables separately for both groups, neither the whole group nor one of the groups was used as a reference group. Thus, simultaneous multiple-sample analysis was not used.

Finally, it was decided to proceed with structural modeling instead of more exploratory factor analyses with the test taker characteristics and the tests for both groups separately. However, as a final check, exploratory factor analysis of the twelve test taker characteristics (now reduced from the earlier sixteen) for both groups showed that an uncorrelated four-factor solution that reflected the content of the items was the most parsimonious and interpretable.

Research questions

These research questions were generally based on the substantive literature in the field of language testing and SLA as well as the general research questions of this study outlined in Chapter 1. Four specific questions were investigated in all the models in both the non Indo-European and the Indo-European groups. Each of these questions was concerned with one of the test taker characteristics and one or more test performance factors. It should be noted that these research questions were posed in the form of questions and not in the form of hypotheses. This was in keeping with the philosophical perspective used in this study, which was to explore the relationships among the variables rather than to confirm or reject hypotheses.

Question 1 (Q1): Question 1 was concerned with the influence of home country formal instruction on test performance. It took the following form: Does home country formal instruction positively influence the reading and writing factors (RW1 and RW2) of the tests? A supplementary question that was asked was: Would this influence be stronger on the subjects of the non Indo-European group than on the Indo-European group because the non Indo-European group might have no other form of instruction and exposure to English? This question was asked due to a widely held belief that Indo-European group subjects could use their own native languages to facilitate their learning of English through creative understanding in a familiar language (for example, similar sentence structures, similar reading and writing structures, familiar cognates) as well as the common Roman script in the Indo-European language family (and western culture).

Question 2 (Q2): This question was concerned with the influence of home country informal instruction on test performance. It took the following form: Does home country informal instruction positively influence the listening and speaking (LS1 and LS2) factors of the tests? An additional question that was asked was: Would this influence be stronger on the subjects of the Indo-European group than the non Indo-European group? This question was asked as it is widely thought that the former group could make use of known patterns of speaking more effectively (for example, greetings, turn taking, conversation) that are similar to the Indo-European language family (and western culture).

Question 3 (Q3): This question was concerned with the influence of English speaking country instruction on test performance. It took the following form: Does English speaking country formal instruction and informal exposure positively influence the listening and speaking (LS1 and LS2) factors of the tests? Since it is unclear whether these factors influence one group more than the other, no additional question was asked.

Question 4 (Q4): This question was concerned with the influence of monitoring on test performance. It took the following form: Does monitoring positively influence the reading and writing (RW1 and RW2) factors of the tests and negatively influence the listening and speaking (LS1 and LS2) factors of the tests? This question was asked as the tests that constitute the listening and speaking mode constructs are speeded tests unlike the reading and writing tests, and, therefore, there would not be sufficient time for monitoring.

It has also been hypothesized by Krashen (1985) that language learners who **acquire** a language (through informal instruction) do not monitor the new language as much as language learners who **learn** the new language (through formal instruction). This hypothesis could not be directly tested here as we do not clearly know what kind of instruction the non Indo-European and Indo-European groups have had previous to this study. However Table 3.9 shows that the non Indo-European group received more home country formal instruction than the Indo-European group (items BQ07, 09, and 10) and that the Indo-European group received more home country informal instruction and English speaking country instruction (items 15, 17, 20, 23, 28). It can therefore be hypothesized that since the non Indo-European group received, in general, more formal instruction and that the Indo-European group received, in general, more informal instruction, the non Indo-European group can be expected to monitor more than the Indo-European group. Thus, in addition, to Q4, an additional question which was asked was: Would the influence of monitoring on test performance be stronger for the non Indo-European group than the Indo-European group?

Other questions not central to this study but related to the relationships among the test taker characteristics formulated were: Would home country formal be negatively related to home country informal for both the non Indo-European and the Indo-European groups? Similarly, would English speaking country be negatively related to home country formal for both non Indo-European and Indo-European groups? And, would home country informal be positively related to monitoring? All these questions are illustrated in Figure 3.1. The positive (+) and the negative (-) signs associated with the specific research questions in Figure 3.1 indicate that the research question is positive or negative.

Figure 3.1

Research questions illustrated for both the non Indo-European and Indo-European groups

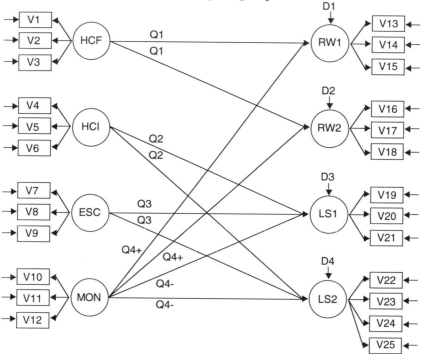

Structural models

The structural models that incorporated the four specific research questions were as follows.

Model 1 (Equal influence factors model)

This model posited common, equal and direct influences of all test taker characteristics on test performance factors, and could be termed the **Equal influence factors model**. In this model, all the four test taker characteristic factors, home country formal, home country informal, English speaking country, and monitoring were set up to have equal influences on the four test performance factors that were used in this study, the two reading and writing factors (RW1 and RW2) and the two listening and speaking factors (LS1 and LS2). Figure 3.2 represents this Basic Model 1, in which the single directional arrows show how theoretically all the four test taker characteristics could influence the four test performance factors equally and directly.

Figure 3.2

**Structural representation of Basic Model 1: Equal influence factors
model**

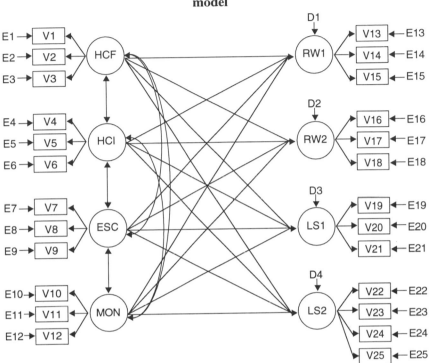

Model 2 (Gardner's intervening factors model)

This model was based on Gardner's (1985) socio-educational model and is
referred to hereafter as Gardner's intervening factors model. Gardner posits the
social milieu as the first group of variables (cultural beliefs), followed by
individual difference variables (intelligence, language aptitude, motivation, and
situational anxiety), then followed by SLA contexts (formal and informal
language training), and finally linguistic and non-linguistic outcomes.

Model 2 posited that the exposure variables home country formal, home
country informal, and English speaking country (which are analogous to
Gardner's SLA contexts) influence monitoring (not included in Gardner's
model) which in turn influences test performance (Gardner's linguistic outcomes). Figure 3.3 represents this Basic Model 2, in which all the three
instruction/exposure factors influence monitoring directly, and then this factor
goes on to directly influence the four test performance factors. The figure does
not show all the direct influences that are possible, for example, influences from
the exposure/instruction factors to the test performance without the intervening
factor of monitoring.

Since this study explored the relationships among test taker characteristics and test performance, variations based on these two basic models were explored. This was done by changing the model specifications of the basic models using both model fit statistics and substantive theory.

Figure 3.3

Structural representation of Basic Model 2: Gardner's intervening factors model

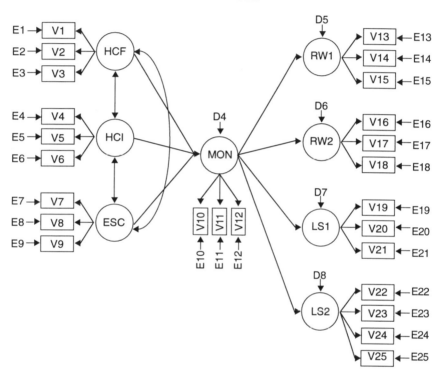

Basic Models 1 and 2 (represented in Figures 3.2 and 3.3 respectively) show the 25 observed variables, V1 to V25, represented in rectangles; the eight (or nine) factors, both independent and dependent, F1 to F8, (and F9 when the G factor was used) represented in circles; the errors of the observed variables are E1 to E25 and the disturbances of the dependent factors are D5 to D8 (and D9 when F9 was used). Table 3.11 presents the names, labels and descriptions of all variables and factors for Basic Models 1 and 2.

Table 3.11

Names, labels, and descriptions of variables and constructs in Basic Models 1 and 2

Variable/factor	Label	Description
V1	BQ07	Item 7: Home country formal instruction
V2	BQ09	Item 9: ditto
V3	BQ10	Item 10: ditto
V4	BQ14	Item 14: Home country informal instr./exposure
V5	BQ15	Item 15: ditto
V6	BQ17	Item 17: ditto
V7	BQ20	Item 20: English speaking country instr./expos.
V8	BQ23	Item 23: ditto
V9	BQ28	Item 28: ditto
V10	BQ39	Item 39: Monitoring
V11	BQ40	Item 40: ditto
V12	BQ41	Item 41: ditto
V13	FCE1	FCE Paper 1- reading comprehension
V14	FCE2	FCE Paper 2 - composition
V15	FCE3	FCE Paper 3 - use of English
V16	TOEFL2	TOEFL Section 2 - structure & written expression
V17	TOEFL3	TOEFL Section 3 - vocabulary & reading compr.
V18	TEW	Test of English Writing
V19	FCE4	FCE Paper 4 - listening comprehension
V20	FCE5	FCE Paper 5 - face-to-face oral interview
V21	TOEFL1	TOEFL Section 1 - listening comprehension
V22	SPK COMP	SPEAK Comprehensibility
V23	SPK GRAM	SPEAK Grammar
V24	SPK PRON	SPEAK Pronunciation
V25	SPK FLCY	SPEAK Fluency
F1	HCF	Home country formal instruction
F2	HCI	Home country informal instruction/exposure
F3	ESC	English speaking country instruction/exposure
F4	MON	Monitoring
F5	RW1	Reading-writing Factor 1- FCE papers 1,2,3
F6	RW2	Reading-writing Factor 2- TOEFL sections 2,3; TEW
F7	LS1	Listening-speaking Factor 1- interactional; FCE 4,5; TOEFL 1
F8	LS2	Listening-speaking Factor 2- non-interactional; SPEAK
F9	G	General factor

Note: E1 to E25 are associated with V1 to V25; and D4 or D5 to D8 (and D9) are associated with F4 or F5 to F8 (and F9).

4 Modeling the data: The results of the study

Overview

This chapter presents the results of modeling the multi-group data. Before investigating the relationships among the test taker characteristics and test performance, test taker characteristics and test performance were modeled separately. Then, two models that were based on the two basic models presented in the previous chapter were evaluated. Summary goodness-of-fit statistics, standardized estimates for parameters, and explanations for the four research questions are presented and evaluated.

Modeling test taker characteristics

An exploratory factor analysis of the four test taker characteristics (home country formal, home country informal, English speaking country, monitoring) found that a four-factor orthogonal solution was parsimonious and very interpretable for single-group data. Summary statistics of this analysis were presented in the previous chapter. Based on this result, a four-factor model with some correlations among the four constructs for the twelve observed variables was designed for multiple-group data, that is, for both the non Indo-European and the Indo-European groups. These constructs represented the four test taker characteristics with paths from each of them to each of the three observed variables associated with the constructs. Correlations among home country formal and English speaking country, home country formal and monitoring, English speaking country and monitoring were designed in the model. Figure 4.1 displays this model for both groups.

Table 4.1 presents the results of the modeling for the two groups. Judging from the χ^2 statistic as well as all other indices, the model fits well for the non Indo-European group and not as well for the Indo-European group. The statistical fit, however, is not significant ($p < .057$) even for the non Indo-European group. But, since the other fit indices indicated a good fit for both groups and this supplemented the exploratory factor analysis results for the single group, it was decided to use this model in the modeling of test taker characteristics and test performances later.

Figure 4.1

**Modeling test taker characteristics: Model for the non Indo-European
and the Indo-European group**

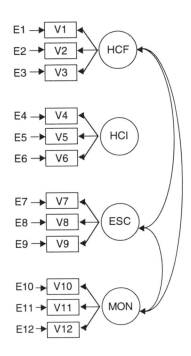

Table 4.1

**Goodness-of-fit indices for modeling test taker characteristics for both
groups**

Index	Non Indo-European	Indo-European
χ^2	67.90	190.82
df	51	51
p <	0.057	0.001
χ^2 / df	1.33	3.74
SB χ^2	67.85	181.18
BBNFI	0.95	0.89
BBNNFI	0.98	0.90
CFI	0.99	0.92

Notes: SB χ^2 = Satorra-Bentler scaled χ^2; BBNFI = Bentler-
Bonett normed fit index; BBNNFI = Bentler-Bonett
nonnormed fit index; CFI = comparative fit index

Figures 4.2 and 4.3 present the standard estimates for paths for the non Indo-European and the Indo-European groups respectively. The individual path coefficients for the observed variables are uniformly high though somewhat different for both groups. Further, the correlations among the constructs are different between home country formal and English speaking country (-.249 for the non Indo-European and .093 for the Indo-European group) and home country formal and monitoring (.205 for the non Indo-European and .138 for the Indo-European group) and similar in strength between English speaking country and monitoring (-.221 for the non Indo-European and -.227 for the Indo-European group). But when these figures are taken together with the goodness-of-fit statistics presented in Table 4.1, these estimates show that this measurement model is an acceptable model for the data for both the non Indo-European and the Indo-European groups.

Figure 4.2

Modeling test taker characteristics: Standardized estimates for paths for the non Indo-European group

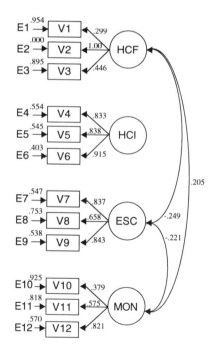

Figure 4.3

Modeling test taker characteristics: Standardized estimates for paths for the Indo-European group

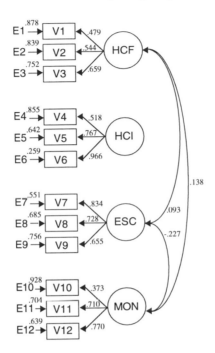

Modeling test performance

An exploratory factor analysis of test performance conducted by Bachman *et al.* (1995) suggested a higher-order general factor and four first-order factors for single-group data. Summarized results of this analysis were presented in the previous chapter. Based on these results a model with a higher-order general factor (HOF) with four first-order factors was designed for multiple-group data, that is, for the non Indo-European and the Indo-European groups. Figure 4.4 displays the paths from the HOF to the four first-order factors and their relationships with the thirteen observed variables.

The basic model displayed in Figure 4.4 failed to provide a convergent likelihood solution within 250 iterations for either the non Indo-European or the Indo-European group. Several refinements to the basic model were attempted for both groups but still the problem of convergence remained. Therefore, it seemed as though there were fundamental problems in the data with respect to the higher-order general factor model being estimated despite evidence to the

Figure 4.4

Modeling test performance: Higher-order general factor model for both the non Indo-European and the Indo-European groups

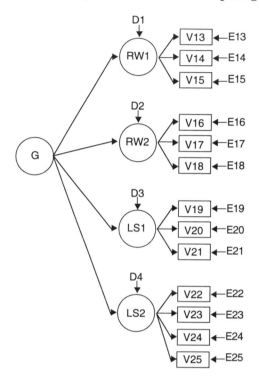

contrary from Bachman *et al.*'s (1995) exploratory factor analysis results which suggested a higher-order general factor model with four first-order factors. Two explanations that could be offered for this difference are: first, while Bachman *et al.*'s study was based on single-group data (N=1448), this study used multiple-group data (Non Indo-European and Indo-European groups), and second, while the former study used a large sample size (1448), this study used smaller sample sizes (380 and 605). Though these sample sizes are larger than Boomsma's (1987) cautionary sample size of 200 for nonconverging solutions, it is possible that the sample sizes used in this study were not sufficiently large. Thus, it was felt that an alternative approach to fitting test performance should be attempted.

The alternative approach attempted was the nested factor model proposed by Gustafsson and Balke (in press); also known as the bi-factor model (see Rindskopf and Rose 1988). In this approach, there would be one general factor with a relationship to all observed variables directly along with the four first-order factors having a narrow range of influence over the observed variables associated with them. Thus, the four first-order factors are nested within the general factor, giving it the name nested factor model. Figure 4.5 displays the nested factor model for the thirteen observed variables.

In the modeling of the nested factor model for both groups, a major problem of identification was encountered: the parameter estimates of the general factor were said to have become in EQS language "linearly dependent on other parameters". This is another way of stating that the covariance matrix of the parameter estimate is singular with the parameter as estimated being a linear combination of other parameters. As a result of this problem of model under-identification, the goodness-of-fit of the model to the data is indeterminate. Thus, this approach to modeling test performance factors did not produce model fit.

Figure 4.5

Modeling test performance: Nested factor model for the non Indo-European and the Indo-European group

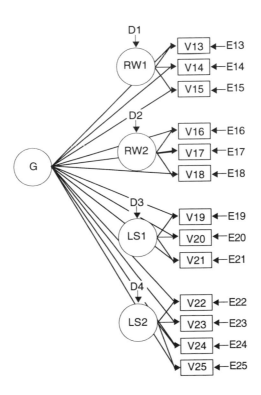

A third approach to modeling test performance was then attempted: this was a correlated four-factor model. The motivation for this model came from the exploratory factor analysis results from Bachman *et al.* (1995) which suggested a higher-order general factor and four first-order factors. Further, modeling in language testing research (for example, Bachman and Palmer 1981) has shown that when a higher-order factor with first-order factors is the best explanation, a correlated first-order factor (without the higher-order factor) solution is not an unsatisfactory explanation either. Figure 4.6 displays the model for the thirteen observed variables with four correlated factors. Modeling test performance using this approach was successful.

Figure 4.6

Modeling test performance: Correlated factor model for the Non Indo-European and the Indo-European group

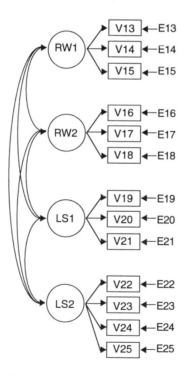

Table 4.2 presents the results of the modeling for the two groups. Judging only from the χ^2 and the χ^2/df statistics, the model was not a very good one. However, the other fit indices, especially the CFI, indicated that the model fits quite well for both the non Indo-European and the Indo-European groups.

Figures 4.7 and 4.8 present the standard estimates for paths for the non Indo-European and the Indo-European groups respectively. These individual path coefficients of the observed variables were uniformly high (.500 and higher) for both groups. The correlations though once again very high (.500 and higher) were uniformly lower for the Indo-European group except for the correlation between LS1 and LS2 (.705 for the non Indo-European and .735 for the Indo-European group). When these figures were taken into account with the goodness-of-fit indices, the statistical lack of fit did not become an obstacle in accepting this model as a reasonably good measurement model for test performance for both groups.

Figure 4.7

Modeling test performance: Standardized estimates for paths for the non Indo-European group

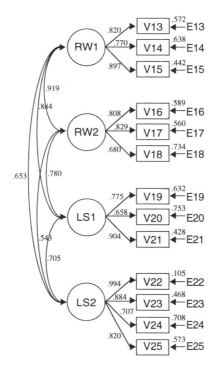

Table 4.2

Goodness-of-fit indices for modeling test performance for both groups

Index	non Indo-European	Indo-European
χ^2	221.70	205.66
df	59	59
p <	0.001	0.001
χ^2/df	3.76	3.49
SB χ^2	220.78	202.45
BBNFI	0.94	0.95
BBNNFI	0.94	0.95
CFI	0.95	0.97

Notes: SB χ^2 = Satorra-Bentler scaled χ^2; BBNFI = Bentler-Bonett normed fit index; BBNNFI = Bentler-Bonett nonnormed fit index; CFI = comparative fit index

Figure 4.8

Modeling test performance: Standardized estimates for paths for the Indo-European group

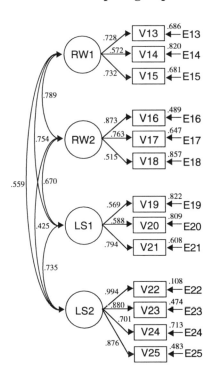

Test taker characteristics and test performance factors

Modeling relationships among test taker characteristics and test performance was based on the results of modeling the two groups of factors separately. Since the four-factor model of the test taker characteristics and the four-factor model of the test performance fit the data for both groups, the first basic model that was attempted for modeling was one that had four factors for each of the two groups of factors.

Model 1

This model was based on the Equal influence factors model presented in the previous chapter as the Basic Model 1. Model 1, which is displayed in Figure 4.9, had 25 variables grouped into four independent factors, home country formal (HCF), home country informal (HCI), English speaking country (ESC), and monitoring (MON), and four dependent factors, RW1, RW2, LS1, and LS2.

Raw data were read in and this produced univariate statistics: coefficients of skewness and kurtosis for the 25 variables were mostly in the range -0.6 to 0.6 for the non Indo-European (NIE) group and the range -0.8 to 0.7 for the Indo-European (IE) group, indicating that the distribution was close to normal. However, once again, multivariate kurtosis showed positive kurtosis (normalized estimate: 16.4 for the NIE group and 13.6 for the IE group). Again, these estimates indicated that the distribution was only in moderate violation of multivariate normality, suggesting that the maximum likelihood with ROBUST estimation procedure should be used.

Model specification began with specifying paths among all test taker characteristic factors and test performance factors based on the hypotheses and substantive theory. Therefore, all independent factors that were posited to have influence on all dependent factors along with free correlations among the test taker characteristics and the test performances were designed, producing a saturated or a basic model. Refinements of this basic model based on the Wald and Lagrange tests as well as substantive theory followed. Finally, when the search for the most parsimonious and interpretable models was completed for both groups, the models were examined and compared since they were all nested (Bollen 1989).

Table 4.3 presents the χ^2 statistics for the basic and restricted models for the two groups. These models differed in the numbers of paths specified from the independent factors to the dependent factors. Figures and standard estimates for paths for all these models (other than the Basic Model and Model 1A) are presented in Appendix 3. For the NIE group, apart from the Basic Model, only one model converged (Model 1A); the other models had nonconverging solutions even after 250 iterations. For the IE group, apart from the Basic Model, three models (Models 1A, 1B and 1C) converged. The χ^2 and the χ^2/df ratio indicated that the 1A models for the NIE group and the IE group were the best. And, as Table 4.3 shows, the χ^2 difference increased from 1A to 1B and from 1B to 1C. Thus, these two 1A models for the NIE and the IE groups were examined in detail.

Table 4.3

Model 1: Goodness-of-fit of models for both groups*

Model	Group	Model fit χ^2	df	χ^2/df	Change χ^2 diff.	df diff.
Basic	NIE	518.39	247	2.10	-	-
1A	NIE	577.66	258	2.24	-	-
Basic	IE	751.19	247	3.04	-	-
1A	IE	767.12	258	2.97	-	-
1B	IE	793.42	259	3.06	26.30	1
1C	IE	798.68	258	3.10	5.26	-1

*Note: Probabilities for all models were less than .001

Table 4.4 presents the goodness-of-fit indices for the 1A models for both groups. While the χ^2/df ratio for both groups was relatively high, the NIE group was better (2.24). This indicated that the model for the NIE group fitted the data for that group better than did the model for the IE group. Although the p values for both models (p < 0.001) indicated that there was lack of statistical fit of data to the models, the other fit indices seemed to show a reasonably good model fit with the comparative fit index particularly high for both groups (0.94 for the NIE group and 0.92 for the IE group).

Examination of standardized path coefficients for paths between independent factors and dependent factors presented in Table 4.5 and Figures 4.9 and 4.10 showed differences between the two groups: two path estimates for each of the two groups did not have counterparts in the other group as they were dropped based on the Wald Test. In the NIE group, the influence of monitoring on RW1 is .223 but the corresponding path for the IE group was not significant. Similarly, for the IE group, the influence of English speaking country on RW1 was .217 while the corresponding path for the NIE group was not significant. Other noticeable differences between the two groups included the following:
1 the influence of home country formal on LS1 (.135 for the NIE group and -.348 for the IE group) and
2 the influence of monitoring on RW2 (-.243 for the NIE group and .047 for the IE group).

However, there was one influence that was of comparable strength for both groups: the influence of English speaking country on LS1 (.231 for the NIE group and .226 for the IE group).

Table 4.4
Goodness-of-fit indices for Model 1A

Index	non Indo-European	Indo-European
χ^2	577.66	767.12
df	258	258
p <	0.001	0.001
χ^2/df	2.24	2.97
SB χ^2	568.07	754.38
BBNFI	0.89	0.88
BBNNFI	0.93	0.90
CFI	0.94	0.92

Notes: SB χ^2 = Satorra-Bentler scaled χ^2; BBNFI = Bentler-Bonett normed fit index; BBNNFI = Bentler-Bonett nonnormed fit index; CFI = comparative fit index.

Table 4.5

Model 1A: Standardized path coefficients for paths between factors for both groups*

	HCF	HCI	ESC	MON	R^2
RW1				**.223**	**.049**
	-.163		.217		.072
RW2		**-.128**		**-.243**	**.076**
	-.127			.047	.018
LS1	**.135**	**.082***	**.231**		**.078**
	-.348	.130	.226		.188
LS2	**-.105***	**.126**	**.176**		**.057**
	-.191		.227		.088

*Notes: Blank space indicates influence was not estimated or significant; NIE group estimates are in the first line (also in bold) and IE group estimates are in the second line; all estimates are significant at p < .01 or t > 2.58 except estimates with an asterisk which are significant at p < .05 or t > 1.96; the disturbances of dependent factors were correlated but are not shown here.

Figure 4.9

Model 1A: Standardized estimates for paths for the non Indo-European group

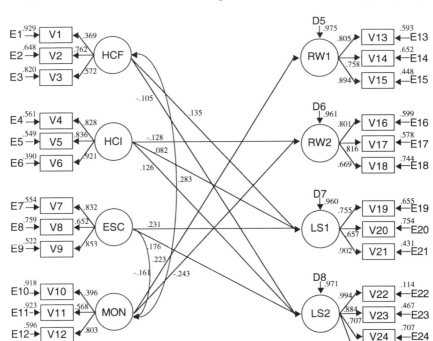

The R^2 statistic from Table 4.5 (which is the squared multiple correlation coefficient obtained by subtracting 1 from the standard residual variable in a recursive model) showed that not very much of the variance of the dependent factors was accounted for by the independent factors. For both groups the R^2 statistic was rather low: the highest was .188 for LS1 (IE group) and the lowest .018 for RW2 (IE group). The average R^2 for the NIE group was .065 (about 7%) and for the IE group was 0.092 (about 9%). While the figure for the non IE group was about the same, the IE had a little more accounted for in this model.

Explanation for the four research questions

This analysis also provided explanations for the four specific research questions asked earlier. The answer to Question 1 was **mixed**: there was no influence from HCF on RW1 and RW2 for the NIE group but there was one negative influence for the IE group, HCF on RW1 (-.163). Thus, the answer to the first research question is negative, that is, home country formal instruction does not positively influence the reading and writing factors (RW1 and RW2) for both groups. However, for the NIE group, HCF had negative influence on LS2 (-.105), and for

Figure 4.10

Model 1A: Standardized estimates for paths for the Indo-European group

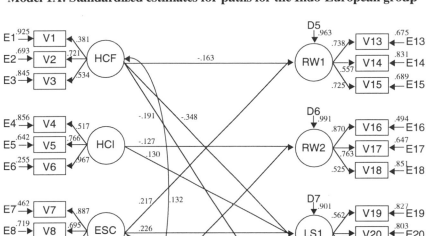

the IE group, HCF had negative influence on LS1 (-.348) and LS2 (-.191). Thus, though HCF did not have clear positive influence on RW1 and RW2, there was sufficient evidence to indicate that there was substantive negative influence on the listening and speaking (LS1 and LS2) factors.

The answer to Question 2 was a **weak yes** as there was some influence from HCI on LS1 (.082 for the NIE group and .130 for the IE group), and on LS2 (.126 for the NIE group). In addition, for both groups, HCI had negative influences on RW2 (-.128 for the NIE group and -.127 for the IE group). Though this was not a direct answer to the question, it indicates that RW2 is very different from the listening and speaking factors (especially LS1).

There was a **strong yes** to Question 3 as ESC seemed to influence LS1 strongly (.231 for the NIE group and .226 for the IE group) and LS2 (.176 for the NIE group and .227 for the IE group).

The answer to Question 4 was **mixed** as the influences were **mixed** for the NIE group. The influence of MON on RW1 was strongly positive (.223) but it was strongly negative on RW2 (-.243). For the IE group, on the other hand, there was a weak positive influence, MON on RW2 (.047).

Reasonable explanation versus statistical fit

From the results presented above for Model 1s, it was apparent that the models did not produce either a clear overall statistical fit or lack of fit for both groups so that they could be either accepted or rejected in terms of statistical significance. The comparative fit indices (0.94 for the NIE group and 0.92 for the IE group), however, showed that the models provided reasonably good explanations of the data. Therefore, it was thought that the results should be examined further so that if the models provided a reasonably good explanation of the relationships among the factors for both groups, they could be accepted. The examination showed the following:

1 for the NIE group: while the average absolute standardized residuals were 0.07 and the residuals were normally distributed, the errors for each of the variables were between .390 to .929 (with one exception of E22=.114); the disturbances for each of the dependent factors were between .960 and .975 (these figures are used to compute R^2: $1-D^2$) and correlations between them were .614 to .916; (these correlations are presented in Appendix 2);

2 for the IE group: while the average absolute standardized residuals were 0.04 and the residuals were normally distributed, the errors for each of the variables were between .462 to .925 (with the exception of E22=.109, and E6=.255); the disturbances for each of the dependent factors were between .901 and .991 and correlations between them were .442 to .828; (these correlations are presented in Appendix 2).

While the standardized residuals and their distribution seemed to suggest that the models might be close to a fit for both groups, there were some discouraging signs: the high errors indicated considerable measurement error in the variables and the high disturbances indicated that the amount of variance accounted for (R^2) in each of the structural equations was quite low, which means a low proportion of variance in the dependent factors was accounted for by the independent factors. Therefore, since the overall fits of the models to the data were not clearly acceptable and these figures discussed above seemed to diagnose weaknesses in the fit of the models, it was decided to evaluate Model 2.

Model 2

Model 2 is a variation of Gardner's (1985) socio-educational model, introduced in the previous chapter as basic Model 2 (or Gardner's intervening factors model) and displayed in the previous chapter in Figure 3.3. In this model there were 25 variables grouped into three kinds of constructs: HCF, HCI and ESC (previous exposure to English); MON (Monitoring), and RW1, RW2, LS1 and LS2 (test performance factors). In this model HCF, HCI and ESC were independent factors, MON was a dependent and an intervening factor, and RW1, RW2, LS1 and LS2 were dependent factors. The paths, therefore, from the independent factors to the dependent factors could be drawn directly to them or through the intervening factor providing for both direct and/or indirect influences.

Univariate and multivariate statistics were the same as those presented for Models 1s for both groups, so maximum likelihood with ROBUST estimation procedure was used for Model 2 as well. Model specification began with specifying paths from all the exposure factors to the Monitoring factor and from this factor to each of the test performance factors, along with free correlations among all the test taker characteristics and the test performances, providing a saturated or basic model. Refinements on this basic model for the two groups based on the Wald and Lagrange tests as well as substantive theory followed. Finally, when the search for the most parsimonious and interpretable models was completed for both groups, the models were examined and compared since they were all nested.

Table 4.6 presents the χ^2 statistics for the basic and restricted models for the two groups. These models differed in the numbers of paths, both direct and indirect, that led from the exposure factors to the intervening factor of monitoring, and then on to the test performance factors. Figures and standardized estimates for paths for all the models (other than the basic model and Models 2A) are presented in Appendix 4. Of the models evaluated, the best fitting models judging from the χ^2 and χ^2/df ratio statistics seemed to be Models 2A for both groups: χ^2=556.38 and χ^2/df=2.17 for the NIE group and χ^2=779.64 and χ^2/df=3.01 for the IE group. The χ^2 differences also indicated that Models 2A for both groups were the best fitting ones though Model 2A for the NIE group had a better fit to the data than Model 2A for the IE group. A detailed analysis of these two models for each group follows.

Table 4.6

Model 2: Goodness-of-fit of models for both groups*

		Model fit			Change	
Model	Group	χ^2	df	χ^2/df	χ^2 diff.	df diff.
Basic	NIE	518.39	247	2.10	-	-
2A	NIE	556.38	257	2.17	-	-
2B	NIE	574.61	258	2.23	18.23	1
2C	NIE	576.29	259	2.23	1.68	1
2D	NIE	578.78	259	2.24	2.49	0
Basic	IE	751.19	247	3.04	-	-
2A	IE	779.64	259	3.01	-	-
2B	IE	788.35	261	3.02	8.71	2
2C	IE	789.39	261	3.02	1.04	0
2D	IE	811.82	262	3.10	22.43	1

Note: Probabilities for all models were less than .001

Table 4.7 presents the goodness-of-fit indices for the Models 2A for both groups. For the NIE group, the χ^2/df ratio was still above the 2.0 estimate for acceptability, and for the IE group, the ratio was too high and well above the figure for an acceptable model fit. The other fit indices were almost the same for both groups as those for Model 1 presented in table 4.4. And, as did Models 1A, these two models lacked statistical fit (p < 0.001).

Table 4.7

Model 2A: Goodness-of-fit indices for both groups

Index	non Indo-European	Indo-European
χ^2	556.38	779.64
df	257	259
p <	0.001	0.001
χ^2/df	2.17	3.01
$SB\chi^2$	398.77	558.78
BBNFI	0.90	0.88
BBNNFI	0.93	0.90
CFI	0.94	0.92

Notes: SB χ^2 = Satorra-Bentler scaled χ^2; BBNFI = Bentler-Bonett normed fit index; BBNNFI = Bentler-Bonett nonnormed fit index; CFI = comparative fit index.

Examination of the Direct (D), Indirect (I) and Total (T) influences of the exposure factors (HCF, HCI and ESC) on the intervening factor (MON) and the four exposure factors directly on the dependent factors (RW1, RW2, LS1 and LS2) for both groups was done so that the structure of the models could be interpreted better. Figures 4.11 and 4.12 illustrate these influences for the NIE and the IE groups respectively.

Influences on test performance factors: Non Indo-European group

As presented in Table 4.8 and Figure 4.11, for the NIE group, each of the exposure factors had direct (D) influences on at least two of the test performance factors. The exposure factor with the strongest direct influence was HCF with direct influence on both of the reading-writing test factors: RW1 (.226) and RW2 (.289); on one of the two listening-speaking test factors: LS1 (.319); and on MON (.266). HCI had moderate direct influence on both the listening-speaking test factors: LS1 (.105) and LS2 (.141), while ESC had direct influence on both the two listening-speaking factors: LS1 (.246) and LS2 (.164) but negative influence on MON (-.142). MON had direct influence on both the reading-writing factors: RW1 (.186) and RW2 (.183).

Indirect (I) influences which were the products (or sums of products) of direct influences were few in number and generally weak, as shown in Table 4.8: HCF on RW1 (.050) and RW2 (.049) and ESC on RW1 (-.026) and RW2 (-.026).

In terms of total (T) influence, as shown in Table 4.8, there were at least five noteworthy positive influences, in order of magnitude: HCF on RW2 (.338), on LS1 (.319), on RW1 (.276) and on MON (.266); and ESC on LS1 (.246). Other noticeable influences were: MON on RW1 (.186) and on RW2 (.183).

Table 4.8

Model 2A: Direct (D), Indirect (I) and Total (T) influences on test performances for the non Indo-European group*

	HCF	HCI	ESC	MON	R^2
MON					
D	.266		-.142*		
I					
T	.266		-.142*		.109
RW1					
D	.226			.186	
I	.050*		-.026		
T	.276		-.026	.186	.110
RW2					
D	.289			.183	
I	.049		-.026		
T	.338		-.026	.183	.150
LS1					
D	.319	.105	.246		
I					
T	.319	.105	.246		.137
LS2					
D		.141	.164		
I					
T		.141	.164		.047

*Blank space indicates influence was not estimated or significant; all direct and total influence estimates are significant at $p < .01$ or $t > 2.58$ except the estimate with asterisk which is significant at $p < .05$ or $t > 1.96$; among indirect influences, only the estimate with asterisk is significant at $p < .05$ or $t > 1.96$; all other indirect influences are not significant; the disturbances of dependent factors were correlated but are not shown here.

Figure 4.11

Model 2A: Influences of test taker characteristics on test performance factors for the non Indo-European group

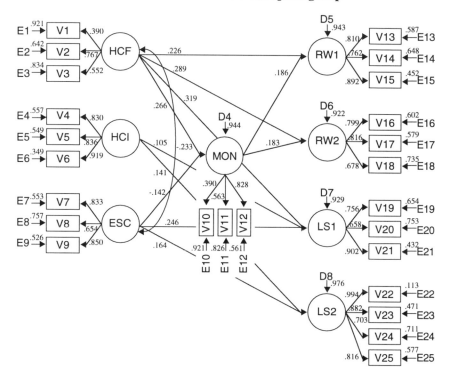

Influences on test performance factors: Indo-European group

As presented in Table 4.9 and Figure 4.12, ESC had direct (D) influence on the three test performance factors: RW1 (.221), LS1 (.216) and LS2 (.212). HCF and HCI, on the other hand, had direct negative influence on three test performance factors: HCF on LS1 (-.205), HCI on RW1 (-.144) and LS2 (-.068). MON was directly influenced differently by HCF and ESC: HCF had a positive direct influence (.160) while ESC had a direct negative one (-.228). MON had weak direct influence on two test performance factors: RW1 (.106) and RW2 (.108).

Indirect (I) influences were once again few in number and generally weak, as shown in Table 4.9: HCF on RW1 (.017), and ESC on RW1 (-.024) and RW2 (-.025).

In terms of total (T) influence, as shown in Table 4.9, there were five notable influences, in order of magnitude: ESC on MON (-.228), on LS1 (.216), on LS2 (.212); HCF on LS1 (-.205) and ESC on RW1 (.197).

Table 4.9

Model 2A: Direct (D), Indirect (I) and Total (T) influences on test performance factors for the IE group*

	HCF	HCI	ESC	MON	R²
MON					
D	.160*		-.228		
I					
T	.160*		-.228		078
RW1					
D		-.144	.221	.106*	
I	.017		-.024		
T	.017	-.144	.197	.106*	.070
RW2					
D				.108*	
I	.017		-.025*		
T	.017		-.025*	.108*	.011
LS1					
D	-.205		.216		
I					
T	-.205		.216		.088
LS2					
D		-.068*	.212		
I					
T		-.068*	.212		.049

*Blank space indicates that influence was not estimated or significant; all direct and total influence estimates are significant at $p < .01$ or $t > 2.58$ except estimates with an asterisk which are significant at $p < .05$ or $t > 1.96$; among indirect influences, only the estimate with an asterisk is significant at $p < .05$ or $t > 1.96$; all other indirect influences are not significant; the disturbances of dependent factors were correlated but are not shown here.

Figure 4.12

Model 2A: Influences of test taker characteristics on test performance factors for the IE group

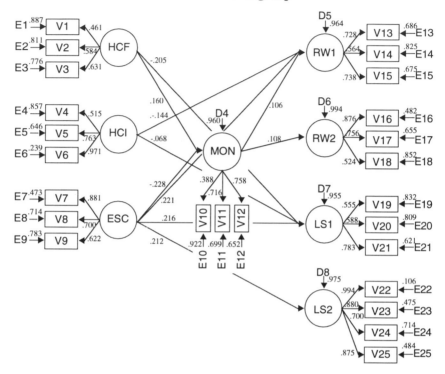

Explanation for the four research questions

This analysis also provided explanations for the four specific research questions asked earlier. The total influence estimates from Tables 4.8 and 4.9 help provide the answers to the questions. For question 1, the answer was mixed. For the non Indo-European group, home country formal strongly influenced test performance factors: on RW1 (.276), RW2 (.338), and LS1 (.319) and MON (.266). For the Indo-European group, however, HCF had negative influence on LS1 (-.205) and weak positive influence on monitoring (.160) and RW1 (.017).

The answer to question 2 was a **weak yes**, as there were weak total influences for the NIE group from home country informal on LS1 (.105) and LS2 (.141). For the IE group, HCI had negative influence on RW1 (-.144) and LS2 (-.068).

The answer to question 3 was again **strong yes**: for the NIE group, English speaking country influenced test performance factors differently on LS1 quite strongly (.246), less strongly on LS2 (.164) but negatively and weakly on RW1 and RW2 (both -.026). In addition, the influence on MON was negative (-.142).

For the IE group too, ESC influenced test performance factors differently: quite strongly on LS1 (.216) and LS2 (.212), and a little less strongly on RW1 (.197), but negatively and weakly on RW2 (-.025). In addition, the influence on MON was negative (-.228).

The answer to Question 4 was a **weak yes**, as there were weak influences: for the NIE group, MON influenced RW1 (.186) and RW2 (.183) and for the IE group, MON influenced the same two test factors: RW1 (.106) and RW2 (.108).

Reasonable explanation versus statistical fit

Once again, from the results presented above for Model 2s, it was apparent that the models did not produce either a clear overall statistical fit or lack of fit for both groups. There was some improvement in model fit from Model 1 for the NIE group and a worse fit from Model 1 for the IE group. Again, however, the comparative fit indices (0.94 for the NIE group and 0.92 for the IE group) showed that the models were quite good. So, a further examination of the results of the Model 2s for the two groups was done as a final check before it was decided whether the models provided a reasonable explanation of the relationships among the factors. The examination showed the following:

1 For the NIE group: while the average absolute standardized residuals were 0.06 and the residuals were normally distributed, the errors for each of the variables were between .349 and .921 (with one exception of E22=.113); the disturbances for each of the dependent factors were between .922 and .976 and correlations between them were .611 to .908; (these correlations are presented in Appendix 2).

2 For the IE group: while the average absolute standardized residuals were 0.05 and the residuals were normally distributed, the errors for each of the variables were between .239 and .922 (with the exception of E22=.106); the disturbances for each of the dependent factors were between .955 and .994 and correlations between them were .435 to .813; (these correlations are presented in Appendix 2).

Again, while the standardized residuals and their distribution seemed to suggest that the models are close to a fit for both groups, there were discouraging signs: the high errors indicated that in the measurement of the variables there was a lot of error, and the high disturbances indicated that the amount of variance accounted for in each of the structural equations was low, which means a very low proportion of variance in the dependent constructs was accounted for by the independent constructs. These results were not very different from the results obtained from the analyses of Models 1. Therefore, since the overall fit of the models to the data was not clearly acceptable and these figures discussed above seemed to diagnose weaknesses in the fit of the models, alternative models were attempted. These are discussed below.

Alternative models

Several alternative models were posited as yet another attempt to find a clearly acceptable model. This was attempted because a common criticism of model formulation and evaluation in structural modeling is that alternative models can be found to explain the data as well (Freedman 1987).

The first alternative model attempted was based on an earlier analysis of these data by Bachman *et al.* (1995). As discussed earlier, treating these data as a single group, Bachman *et al.* showed through an exploratory factor analysis that a higher-order general factor with four first-order factors was the most parsimonious and interpretable factor structure for the data. However, as reported earlier in this chapter, when this model was used to model test performance factors by themselves, there were convergence problems for both groups. Still, it was thought that this might be an alternative model to attempt.

Therefore, a model with a higher-order general factor with four first-order factors for test performance and four test taker characteristic factors was attempted. Modeling with this model was unsuccessful for both groups as all variations of this basic model produced linear dependencies among other parameters. Therefore, this model was considered unacceptable.

A second alternative model that was attempted was the nested factor model proposed by Gustafsson and Balke (in press). As discussed earlier, when this model was attempted with the test performance factors by themselves, there was the problem of linear dependency of the general factor on other parameters. Still, it was considered a possible alternative. While the modeling did not produce any problems, the summary goodness-of-fit statistics showed that this model was not a satisfactory explanation for both groups: for the non Indo-European group, $\chi^2=1037.459$, df=259; χ^2/df=4.01, and for the Indo-European group, $\chi^2=1426.832$, df=260; χ^2/df=5.49.

A third alternative model attempted was a reduced Model 2: exclusion of the monitoring factor, leaving the model with three test taker characteristics and four test performance factors. While this model did not produce any problems, the fit to the data did not improve for both groups: for the non Indo-European group, $\chi^2=457.372$, df=193; χ^2/df=2.37, and for the Indo-European group, $\chi^2=631.404$, df=193; χ^2/df=3.27. In addition to the lack of statistical fit, the parameter estimates were not as strong and less interpretable. Therefore, this model too was considered unacceptable.

As a final attempt at modeling these data, multiple-group analysis was perhaps thought to be the cause of the lack of statistical fit though there was evidence that the two groups were different. These multiple-group data were, therefore, merged so that the data could be treated as a single group. Models 1 and 2 were then used to model these data. The results were as initially expected: treating the two groups as a single group did not improve statistical fit. Summary goodness-of-fit-indices were as follows: for Model 1: $\chi^2=1019.561$, df=257;

χ^2/df=3.97 and for Model 2: χ^2=1047.535, df=260; χ^2/df=4.03. Therefore, these two models were also considered statistically unacceptable even for single-group data.

Summary

In summary, first, two four-factor models were found to be acceptable for the test taker characteristics and the test performance factors for the non Indo-European and the Indo-European groups. Second, two models designed on the equal influence factors model and Gardner's intervening factors model were evaluated for model fit for both groups. While the result of the analysis of Model 1 (the equal influence factors model) was not clearly acceptable, it was close to acceptability for the non Indo-European group. Model 2 (Gardner's intervening factors model) was very interesting for two reasons: model fit for the non Indo-European group was better than for Model 1, and the direct, indirect, and total influences from the test taker characteristics to the test performance factors for both groups were quite substantive and interpretable. Finally, as a last attempt for a clearly acceptable model, three unsuccessful attempts were made with three alternative models (HOF, NF, and a reduced Model 2), and then, the non Indo-European and Indo-European groups were merged into one and analyzed as a single group. None of these attempts produced statistical fit.

5 Discussion of results and conclusions

Overview

The purpose of this study was to investigate the influence of test taker characteristics on EFL test performance by exploring the relationships among test taker characteristics and test performance. It was thought that the variability in EFL test performance in the different skill areas could be examined as a function of test taker characteristics such as previous exposure to English (formal and informal), and self-monitoring of language use. Thus, the general research question and the main substantive issue was to develop an explanatory model which could assess which test taker characteristics influenced test performance and to what extent.

In order to investigate this research question, it was felt that appropriate models which represent the structural relationships between test taker characteristics and test performance factors should be developed so that these models could then be evaluated empirically. The best methodological approach for this is structural modeling as hypothesized relationships among constructs as well as between constructs and observed variables can be represented.

Results of the structural modeling were complicated and extensive, and generally conformed to expectations and the hypotheses. After much exploration, the models provided satisfactory explanations of the data for both the non Indo-European and the Indo-European groups of subjects though they lacked statistical model fit. All test taker characteristic factors made some contribution, direct or indirect, however small, to the test performance factors though the influences differed depending on the native language group. Each of the test taker characteristics, test performance and the research questions associated with each of them are discussed. Model comparisons are also discussed, followed by general conclusions, implications for research and some ideas for further research.

Influence of previous exposure

The three factors of previous exposure or instruction that were used in this study to investigate this influence on EFL test performance were home country formal instruction (HCF), home country informal exposure (HCI) and English speaking country (ESC) instruction or exposure. Their influences were varied and in some cases substantial.

Home country formal instruction

The influence of HCF instruction on the test performance factors in Model 1 for both groups though present, was not substantial. In Model 2 for the non Indo-European group, however, its influence was substantial on three of the test performance factors: RW1, RW2 and LS1. These three factors included the FCE, the TEW, and the TOEFL, but did not include the SPEAK, which makes up the LS2 factor, indicating that HCF instruction was an important factor in performing on the FCE, the TEW and the TOEFL and not on the SPEAK. Since the SPEAK is a non-interactional tape-mediated, speeded, oral test, performance on this test may not benefit very much from formal instruction. This is a notable result especially because HCF instruction did not positively influence any of the test performance factors substantially for the Indo-European group. In fact, there was significant negative influence on LS1 which is made up of TOEFL and FCE listening and oral tests respectively.

Thus, HCF instruction was positively and substantially influential for the NIE group and not for the IE group. While this may not have been entirely unpredictable, it indicates that HCF instruction influences reading, writing and listening performance for EFL learners living in sites where NIE languages are spoken.

In summary, the influence of HCF instruction was more clear in Model 2, where monitoring was an intervening factor. The strong influence of HCF instruction for the NIE group answered question 1 which was whether HCF instruction would positively influence RW1 and RW2. In addition, it answered in the affirmative the supplementary question whether HCF instruction is stronger for the NIE group than the IE group.

Home country informal exposure

HCI exposure did not have as much influence on test performance as HCF instruction for either group across all models. In Model 2, for the NIE group, HCI exposure showed a significant though moderate influence on both the listening-speaking factors. For the IE group, HCI exposure showed negative though moderate influences on two test performance factors, RW1 and LS2.

HCI exposure influence on both the listening-speaking factors for the NIE group is an interesting result. It indicates that informal exposure to English is influential in performance on these two groups of tests: the listening and speaking test parts of the TOEFL and the FCE, (which are interactional) and the SPEAK test (which is non-interactional). Once again, this is not an unpredictable result, as it is commonly thought that informal exposure will help the listening and speaking skill areas, especially for the NIE group. However, the moderate negative influence of HCI exposure on two test performance factors for the IE group is really puzzling; it is not clear why informal exposure would be uninfluential to the IE group.

These results were surprising in terms of what was asked as a research question about HCI exposure. Question 2 asked first whether HCI exposure would positively influence LS1 and LS2 test performance factors, and, next, whether it would show stronger influence on the IE group than the NIE group. The first part of the question was answered in the affirmative by the strong HCI exposure influence on LS1 and LS2 but the second part was just the reverse.

English speaking country instruction or exposure

Although HCF instruction and HCI exposure did have substantial and moderate influence over the test performance factors respectively, neither of them seemed to be as substantive as ESC influence. The influence of ESC instruction or exposure in Model 2 showed substantial positive influences for both groups on LS1 and LS2. In Model 2, for both the NIE and the IE group, there were substantial positive influences on LS1 and LS2 and a not too surprising negative influence on monitoring. For the IE group, there was a moderate influence on RW1 also. The indirect influences were generally low and negative but not significant.

This result confirms a commonly held belief that ESC instruction or exposure is an important influence on performance on listening and speaking skills, that is, a visit to or stay in an English speaking country for pleasure/instruction positively influenced listening and speaking abilities for both groups. In addition, the influence of ESC instruction or exposure on RW1, which is made up of FCE papers 1 to 3, indicates that reading and writing too was positively influenced.

These results showed strong positive answers to the third research question. Question 3 asked whether there would be positive influence of ESC instruction or exposure on LS1 and LS2 for both groups, and that is what the results clearly showed. Thus, this question was answered in the affirmative. However, Question 3 did not ask whether there would be a strong negative influence from ESC instruction or exposure on monitoring for both groups. This will be discussed in the next section.

While these results regarding previous instruction or exposure are not entirely new, there has been little research investigation using these exact categories so that direct comparisons with previous research cannot be made. However, Nation and McLaughlin (1986) in their experimental study of multilingual, bilingual and monolingual learners used two similar conditions of instruction that parallel HCF instruction and HCI exposure: the "explicit learning condition" (with structured presentation and attention on rule-learning) which parallels the HCF instruction and the "implicit learning condition" (with random presentation and no attention on rule-learning) which parallels the HCI exposure. Their results indicate that while the "explicit learning condition" led to greater success for the bilinguals and monolinguals, the learning condition did not make a difference for the multilinguals. This finding contrasts with the results obtained in this study: the performance of the NIE group which was more substantially influenced by HCF instruction was not as good as the IE group on even one of the tests.

Influence of and on monitoring

Monitoring (MON) had a substantial influence on test performance factors for both groups. In the Model 1s for both groups, monitoring had a strong positive influence on RW1 and a negative influence on RW2. This might have been due to the differences in test methods used by the two RW factors. But the Model 2s, which presented MON as an intervening factor, showed more interesting results: HCF instruction had a strong influence on MON and MON had a moderate influence on RW1 and RW2 for both groups (though more for the NIE group).

This result clearly indicates that MON is related to HCF instruction, suggesting that learners who have formal instruction, such as the NIE group, could be the ones who strive for correctness and, therefore, monitor more than those who are more likely to have had more informal learning, and are less concerned with correctness, like the IE group. In addition, it is also interesting to note that MON moderately influenced both the reading and writing tests as both tests provide time enough to respond. Thus, it was unsurprising that since monitoring inhibits output, especially speeded up output like speaking, it did not show any influence on either of the listening and speaking tests.

Also, the influence of ESC instruction or exposure on MON was interesting: the IE group showed more negative influence of ESC instruction or exposure on MON than the non IE group. This result was not unsurprising as the IE group for whom ESC instruction or exposure had greater influence on the tests, monitored their language much less than the NIE group, for whom ESC instruction or exposure had much less influence on the tests.

These results indicate that there is a strong positive relationship between the MON and HCF instruction factors for both groups. More importantly, Krashen's hypothesis that formal learning leads to more monitoring (like the NIE group) and informal learning/acquisition leads to less monitoring (like the IE group) seems to have been supported from these results. This finding must, however, be read in the light of the fact that monitoring in this study was a self-report of monitoring.

EFL test performance

The four EFL test performance factors were modeled as correlated dependent factors. This model was formulated after successful modeling on test performance factors themselves. Unsuccessful modeling of test performance factors included a higher-order general factor and four first-order factors based on Bachman *et al.*'s (1995) exploratory factor analysis. Another model based on Gustafsson and Balke's (in press) nested factor model did not prove successful either. Thus, the four-factor structure with correlated disturbances for test performance was used for all models. This structure did not collapse in any of the modeling; in fact, it did admirably well for both types of models for both groups.

As discussed in Chapter 3, there were two reading-writing factors and two listening-speaking factors. The first two factors, which were the reading-writing factors, could be distinguished by the fact that the variables that made up Reading-Writing 1 were FCE papers 1, 2, and 3 (an FCE written mode); and the variables that made up Reading-Writing 2 were TOEFL sections 2 and 3, and the TEW (an ETS written mode). The listening-speaking factors could be distinguished too: the variables that made up Listening-Speaking 1 were FCE papers 4 and 5, and TOEFL section 1 (an interactional mode); and the variables that made up Listening-Speaking 2 were the SPEAK scores for pronunciation, fluency, grammar, and comprehensibility (a non-interactional mode).

The robustness of this four factor structure across models and groups provides evidence for the following:

1 there was a difference between the FCE and the ETS reading-writing sections, as scores from these two types of tests, though correlated, remained structurally separate;

2 there was a difference between the two kinds of listening-speaking tests: the FCE papers were in an interactional mode and SPEAK (also developed and administered by ETS) was non-interactional in mode. This difference, however, could not be due to the fact that different underlying abilities were being tapped, since Bachman *et al.* (1995) through exploratory factor analysis showed that similar abilities were being measured by both EFL batteries. Thus, it is possible to speculate without the benefit of detailed analyses that the main reason that these factors remained separate though correlated is the use of different test methods in each of the two reading-writing and listening-speaking factors.

More specifically, it is possible that the differences between the two reading-writing factors (RW1 and RW2) were due to the test method and not language ability. The variables that made up RW1 with their corresponding test method were FCE papers 1 (multiple-choice), paper 2 (open-ended), and paper 3 (gap-filling; short completion) as against the variables for RW2, which were TOEFL sections 2 and 3 (both multiple-choice) and TEW (open-ended). The difference between the two factors is clear: there was one test method for each FCE paper (a total of three) but the two TOEFL sections and the TEW together had only two test methods (with multiple-choice in two sections).

Similarly, it is possible that the two listening-speaking factors (LS1 and LS2) were different not because the language ability tapped by the two factors was different but because the test method is different. The variables that made up LS1 were FCE papers 4 (listen to tape and written response; open-ended) and 5 (face-to-face oral interview; oral open-ended) and TOEFL section 1 (listen to tape; written multiple-choice) as against the variables that made up LS2 which were SPEAK (tape-mediated with taped responses). Based on this analysis, it is possible to label the two listening-speaking factors as follows: LS1 as interactional in mode and LS2 non-interactional in mode.

A thorough test method content analysis would have to be conducted before confirming this speculation. Using a detailed instrument such as the one proposed by Bachman (1990) would provide an extension of the construct validation that is normally obtained by examining mere test scores.

Model comparisons

The two models, the equal influence factors model and Gardner's intervening factors model, in which there is a chain of causation with intervening factors, were tested for fit for the two groups. While Model 1 represents the view that previous instruction and exposure to English and self-report of monitoring are equal in status as influences on test performances, Model 2 represents Gardner's (1985) view though he does not include monitoring in any of his models.

Though these two models seem to be clearly different, the results of this study did not show up this difference. For example, in terms of the χ^2/df ratios, for the NIE group, Model 1A was 2.24 and Model 2A was 2.17, and for the IE group, Model 1A was 2.97 and Model 2A was 3.01. In terms of the comparative fit index (CFI), one of the most robust goodness-of-fit indices (Bentler 1990), for the NIE group, for both Models 1A and 2A the value was 0.94, and for the IE group, for both Models 1A and 2A the value was 0.92. The only observable difference between the two groups was that while the indices showed that, for the NIE group, Model 2A was slightly better than Model 1A, for the IE group, it was the other way around: Model 1A was slightly better than 2A. But since the improvement of fit for the NIE group from Model 1A to 2A and the degradation of fit for the IE group from Model 1A to 2A was so small, it is not clear whether the difference in model type was a significant factor.

So, if there is little difference in the results from the two models, then the questions posed by Skehan (1989) about Gardner's (1985) work could be raised again:

> ... *what if MOT were changed in status to make it an exogenous variable at a similar level to INT and ALS? Or what if INT and ALS were combined? Or MOT and ALS reversed? (1989:70)*

Skehan's questions, though specific to Gardner's (1985) work regarding MOT (Motivation), INT (integrative orientation), and ALS (attitude to learning situation), can be used to ask general questions about model formulation: Should these factors be modeled in this order and status? Should these factors be combined or dropped for higher level factors? Should alternative models be formulated for model testing?

These questions could perhaps be answered after more model formulation and evaluation is performed in different academic situations, with different subjects, tests and test taker characteristics.

Conclusions

In conclusion, what is it that can be said of the relationships among test taker characteristics and EFL test performance? And, what can be said of the structural modeling approach used in investigating these relationships?

Without restating the details of the results of this study, it could be said that it is noteworthy that the multiple, complex, subtle and dynamic networks of relationships among test taker characteristics and EFL test performance were uncovered for both groups of subjects (non Indo-European and Indo-European groups). These relationships also indicated that influences on EFL test performance are dependent on many factors working in concert, not a few factors working in isolated ways. And, overall, when this study is replicated with new data and expanded upon with additional variables, then, as Bachman (1990:156) states, test developers and test takers will benefit:

> As research into the effects on test performance of personal attributes and test method facets progresses, test developers will have better information about which characteristics interact with which test method facets, and should be able to utilize this information in designing tests that are less susceptible to such effects, that provide the greatest opportunity for test takers to exhibit their 'best' performance, and which are hence better and fairer measures of the language abilities of interest.

Methodologically, in terms of the structural modeling approach, it is important to point out that for multivariate analyses of dynamic systems like language learning, structural modeling appears to be an essential, if not a preferred, approach. It could be an ideal approach especially if, following Bachman's (1990) proposal, researchers begin to investigate the influence of the four factors that Bachman has identified as ones that influence language test performance. Model formulation and model modification too, especially when done in the exploratory mode of structural modeling, give it a flexibility that other research methodologies do not have. Also, it is noteworthy to point out that, following Cronbach's (1989) proposal, this study followed a "weak" program of construct validation, not one which involved formal hypothesis testing, but one which sought explanations from the many perspectives of the proposed models, hopefully highlighting where the "greatest perplexities lie".

Finally, it is hoped that this study has helped contribute to the beginnings of a theory of construct validation for test performance – a theory that will take into account not only the construct validation of the traits or competencies being measured or the test instruments being used and interpreted, but a theory that will also consider the personal attributes or characteristics of the test takers, the test method facets and random factors, all of which influence language test performance.

Implications for research

This study showed that relationships among test taker characteristics and EFL test performance could be explored using the structural modeling approach. It also showed that a large data set with about 1,000 subjects, 45 background questionnaire items, and thirteen EFL test scores could be modeled successfully.

Further, because reasonable explanations for the relationships could be made, the lack of statistical fit for the models did not seem to be particularly bothersome. This was especially so

1 because the lack of statistical fit was not too bad in all the acceptable models, and
2 because of the fact that the two groups had a fairly large number of cases in them, and the lack of statistical fit could also be due to the large number of cases.

Methodologically, as stated earlier in this section, structural modeling was an adequate and satisfying approach. It provided the scope for model formulation and evaluation from substantive theory as well as from what the data was suggesting.

Future language testing researchers, however, should note that structural modeling is not without its problems. It requires training to program, to interpret and to report. In addition, since the specific programing and terminology differs from EQS to LISREL to LISCOMP, to name a few statistical software programs, it is essential to program extensively with one statistical software before moving to the others.

Other substantial problems also exist especially if there are other kinds of factors involved. First, relationships among test taker characteristics, test method and test performance factors may not be strictly linear for all data. These relationships may in fact be curvilinear. This could be a crucial problem in applied linguistics research especially because linearity of variables is an important assumption in structural modeling. And, because, most researchers who have used structural modeling are language testing and SLA researchers (mainly those working in the Gardner-Giles tradition of social psychology) and their variables are typically linearly related, little is known about variables researched by others.

Second, the measurement of these factors poses another challenge: data collection through questionnaires and self-reports presents problems that may be difficult to deal with and anticipate. For example, self-reports of previous instruction or exposure, as used in this study, could often be somewhat inaccurate because of the subjects' blurring of memory due to a long time lapse or their difficulty in reducing their memory of events into a multiple-choice or Likert type questionnaire.

Third, several hidden relationships between factors and variables could emerge presenting overtly uninterpretable relationships and inexplicable structural models. In these situations, researchers should be informed by substantive theory and previous research results before they begin to use model modification procedures. Otherwise, blind allegiance to statistical suggestions for modifications could result in meaningless relationships.

Fourth, categorical data as opposed to interval data presents an additional challenge for structural modeling and this may require the use of certain statistical software, like LISCOMP (Muthen 1987), for successful modeling.

But, despite these difficulties, structural modeling is a powerful way of investigating the expanded notion of construct validity using the nomothetic span concept.

Further research

Further research along the same lines as this study could include:

1 An improved and simplified background questionnaire and scale development for collection of test taker characteristics, preferably without branching items, would be a great asset for data collection. In addition, self-reported data on other test taker characteristics could be collected. For example, information-processing and cognitive characteristics would be interesting data to add to the already existing group of test taker characteristics. Rose (1978) and Lansman and Hunt (1980) indicate that there is great potential with this line of research, and, therefore, this area of investigation would be worth the extra effort.

2 Content analyses of test method facets would be a valuable addition to test taker characteristics and test performance data. This would bring information of yet another factor that is posited by Bachman (1990) to influence test performance. Research techniques used by Bachman *et al.*, (1988a) and Bachman *et al.* (1991) seem to show promising results and these could be considered.

3 Structural modeling of data that includes an expanded group of test taker characteristics, content analyses of test method facets, and test performance would be a fascinating study. Modeling all these data has not been reported so far, and, therefore, this could be at the cutting edge of language testing research.

4 Modeling data across categorical variables, like gender, native language, race and ethnicity, and using test scores to differentiate ability level groups could add additional dimensions to the substantive research questions and structural modeling. Muthen's (1989b) new approach for investigating factor structure among different groups like the ones mentioned above using the Pearson-Lawley selection formulas is convincing and should be used.

5 Finally, replication of studies with new data could not only build on existing findings but could offer insights that have escaped this researcher as well as others.

Final thoughts

This modeling study provided a unique opportunity to explore the dynamic and complex network of structural relationships among some test taker characteristics and EFL test performance for two primary reasons. First, though only two major test taker characteristics factors were used in these analyses, it was evident that this approach uncovered more information about the relationships of those factors to EFL test performance than would have been possible if these factors were treated individually, or if any other procedure was used. Second, the two native language groups were modeled separately so that the native languages and cultures, and the opportunity to learn English in those two contexts (non Indo-European and Indo-European) could be examined separately. As mentioned earlier, research with additional factors, such as, gender, age, attitude and motivation, learning strategies and styles, to name a few, could provide fuller descriptions. But since not all of these and other test taker characteristics (personal attributes, educational, cognitive, psychological and social characteristics) will have significant influence on test performance, the challenge for language testing researchers is to identify the test taker characteristics that influence test performance and then to model those test taker characteristics with test performance in a network fashion to arrive at a model that could explain the major influences on test performance. A theory of construct validation that includes both content representation and nomothetic span could then emerge.

   To conclude, Upshur (1983) notes that "measurement of individual differences has potential for more direct contributions to theory development in the language sciences" (p. 119). He provides three different aspects for researchers considering the measurement of individual differences and explanation in the language sciences: "establishing a research agenda, elaborating variables and evaluating theoretical models" (p. 119). Three challenges within these aspects are relevant for structural modeling research: incompleteness of structural models (difficulty in knowing whether a model is complete or not), undecidability of best model from available models (difficulty in deciding which and when a model is superior), and inaccuracy in measurement of variables (difficulty in accurately measuring variables, though they may be precisely measured). Finally, since data from the human and language sciences (including language learning and testing) tends to have a great deal of complexity and uncertainty (West and Salk 1987), structural models like the ones examined and discussed in this study may only be scratching at the surface of the complexity. Perhaps, a complex systems analysis, following the example of Pena-Taveras and Cambel (1989), may be required for theory development in the language sciences.

Appendices

1 Background questionnaire
2 Correlations among independent variables (disturbances) of Models 1A and 2A
  Model 1A: NIE Group
  Model 1A: IE Group
  Model 2A: NIE Group
  Model 2A: IE Group
3 Model 1: Figures, standardized estimates for paths and correlations among independent variables
  Model 1B: IE Group
  Model 1C: IE Group
4 Model 2: Figures, standardized estimates for paths and correlations among independent variables
  Model 2B: NIE Group
  Model 2C: NIE Group
  Model 2D: NIE Group
  Model 2B: IE Group
  Model 2C: IE Group
  Model 2D: IE Group
5 EQS computer programing for selected models
6 Correlation matrices for TTCs, TP, and TTCs and TP together for the NIE and IE groups

Appendix 1 Background questionnaire*

(Original English version)

* Only items 1 to 45 were used in this study.

This questionnaire is designed to provide us with information of interest for research purposes. Your answers to these questions will be kept strictly confidential. Please answer each question as accurately as you can. Thank you for your cooperation.

DIRECTIONS:

Please provide the information on the top portion of the answer sheet as instructed. For each question below, darken the appropriate circle on the answer sheet using the pencil provided. All answers should be given on the answer sheet provided. Do not mark anything on this questionnaire.

1 What is your current educational status?
  (A) enrolled in a secondary school
  (B) enrolled part-time in a college, university or other institution of higher education
  (C) enrolled full-time in a college, university or other institution of higher education
  (D) enrolled in a language institute or English course given where I work
  (E) not currently enrolled as a student

2 Have you ever or are you currently taking a course to prepare for the TOEFL?
  (A) yes
  (B) no

3 Have you ever or are you currently taking a course to prepare for the FCE?
  (A) yes
  (B) no

4 Have you ever or are you currently taking a course to prepare for the CPE?
  (A) yes
  (B) no

5 At what age did you begin to learn or use English?
   (A) 1–5 years   (D) 14–17 years
   (B) 6–9 years   (E) 18 or more years
   (C) 10–13 years

6 Have you ever studied English in school or in a language institute in the country you consider to be your home country?
   (A) yes
   (B) no

IF YES, ANSWER QUESTIONS 7–13. IF NO, GO TO QUESTION 13 ON PAGE 3.
7 How many years have you studied English in school or in a language institute?
   (A) less than 1 year   (D) 7–9 years
   (B) 1–3 years   (E) 10 or more years
   (C) 4–6 years

8 How old were you when you first began to study English in school or in a language institute?
   (A) 1–5 years   (D) 14–17 years
   (B) 6–9 years   (E) 18 or more years
   (C) 10–13 years

How many hours per week did you spend in English class ...

9 ... in elementary school?
   (A) none   (D) 7–9 hours
   (B) 1–3 hours   (E) 10 or more hours
   (C) 4–6 hours

10 ... in secondary school?
   (A) none   (D) 7–9 hours
   (B) 1–3 hours   (E) 10 or more hours
   (C) 4–6 hours

11 ... in college and/or language institute?
   (A) none   (D) 7–9 hours
   (B) 1–3 hours   (E) 10 or more hours
   (C) 4–6 hours

12 How many hours are you currently spending in English class?
   (A) none   (D) 7–9 hours
   (B) 1–3 hours   (E) 10 or more hours
   (C) 4–6 hours

13 Have you used English at home with your family or friends in the country you consider to be your home country?
(A) yes
(B) no

IF YES, ANSWER QUESTIONS 14–18. IF NO, GO TO QUESTION 18 ON PAGE 4.

14 How many years have you used English at home?
(A) none
(B) less than 1 year
(C) 1–3 years
(D) 4–6 years
(E) 7 or more years

15 How old were you when you first started to use English at home?
(A) 1–5 years
(B) 6–9 years
(C) 10–13 years
(D) 14–17 years
(E) 18 or more years

16 How much did you use English at home?
(A) not at all
(B) a little
(C) about half the time
(D) most of the time
(E) all the time

17 How much do you currently use English at home?
(A) not at all
(B) a little
(C) about half the time
(D) most of the time
(E) all the time

18 Have you ever learned or used English while visiting or living in an English-speaking country?
(A) yes
(B) no

IF YES, ANSWER QUESTIONS 19–21. IF NO, GO TO QUESTION 30 ON PAGE 6.

19 How old were you when you first went to an English-speaking country?
(A) 1–5 years
(B) 6–9 years
(C) 10–13 years
(D) 14–17 years
(E) 18 or more years

20 How many years in total did you spend there?
   (A) 1 year or less   (D) 8–10 years
   (B) 2–4 years   (E) 11 or more years
   (C) 5–7 years

21 Did you study English in school or in a language institute in the English-speaking country?
   (A) yes
   (B) no

IF YES, ANSWER QUESTIONS 22–27. IF NO, GO TO QUESTION 27 ON PAGE 5.

22 How many years did you study English in school or in a language institute in an English-speaking country?
   (A) less than 1 year   (D) 7–9 years
   (B) 1–3 years   (E) 10 or more years
   (C) 4–6 years

23 How old were you when you first began to study English in school or in a language institute in an English-speaking country?
   (A) 1–5 years   (D) 14–17 years
   (B) 6–9 years   (E) 18 or more years
   (C) 10–13 years

How many hours per week did you spend in English class ...

24 ... in elementary school?
   (A) none   (D) 7–9 hours
   (B) 1–3 hours   (E) 10 or more hours
   (C) 4–6 hours

25 ... in secondary school?
   (A) none   (D) 7–9 hours
   (B) 1–3 hours   (E) 10 or more hours
   (C) 4–6 hours

26 ... in college and/or language institute?
   (A) none   (D) 7–9 hours
   (B) 1–3 hours   (E) 10 or more hours
   (C) 4–6 hours

27 Did you use English at home with family or friends in the English-speaking country?
   (A) yes
   (B) no

IF YES, ANSWER QUESTIONS 28–66. IF NO, GO TO QUESTION 30 ON PAGE 6.

28 How many years did you use English at home with family or friends in the English-speaking country?
   (A) none   (D) 4–6 years
   (B) less than 1 year   (E) 18 or more years
   (C) 1–3 years
29 How old were you when you first started to use English at home in the English-speaking country?
   (A) 1–5 years   (D) 14–17 years
   (B) 6–9 years   (E) 18 or more years
   (C) 10–13 years

The following statements describe some possible reasons why people learn English. For each statement, darken the circle on your answer sheet by the response which is most appropriate for you – i.e., the response which best describes why you want to learn English.

A = strongly agree   (SA)
B = agree   (A)
C = disagree   (D)
D = strongly disagree   (SD)

	SA	A	D	SD
30 I want to be able to read English books, reports, articles, etc. in my field of specialization.	A	B	C	D
31 I want to think and behave as people from America or Great Britain do.	A	B	C	D
32 I want to be able to write professional reports in English.	A	B	C	D
33 I want to fit into an English-speaking community.	A	B	C	D
34 I enjoy learning English as a second or foreign language.	A	B	C	D
35 As an international language, English is useful for communicating with other people whose native language I do not know.	A	B	C	D
36 I want to understand American or British people and culture.	A	B	C	D
37 English is important for career purposes.	A	B	C	D

38 When you hear (or listen to) a mistake in English, do you know it is a mistake because it "sounds" wrong to you, or do you understand why it is wrong?
   (A) Only because it "sounds" wrong.
   (B) Usually because it "sounds" wrong, but sometimes I understand why it is wrong.
   (C) I usually understand why it is wrong.
   (D) I almost always understand why it is wrong.

39 When you see (or read) a mistake in English, do you know it is a mistake because it "looks" wrong to you, or do you understand why it is wrong?
   (A) Only because it "looks" wrong.
   (B) Usually because it "looks" wrong, but sometimes I understand why it is wrong.
   (C) I usually understand why it is wrong.
   (D) I almost always understand why it is wrong.

40 When you speak, do you just say what "sounds" correct, or do you think about the English rules you know?
   (A) I say what "sounds" correct.
   (B) I usually say what "sounds" correct, but sometimes I think about rules.
   (C) I usually think about rules, but I also say what "sounds" correct.
   (D) I always think about rules.

41 When you write, do you just write what "looks" correct or do you think about the English rules you know?
   (A) I write what "looks" correct.
   (B) I usually write what "looks" correct, but sometimes I think about rules.
   (C) I usually think about rules, but I also write what "looks" correct.
   (D) I always think about rules.

How often do you forget to use the English rules you know ...

42 ... in speaking?
   (A) almost always   (C) not very often
   (B) often   (D) almost never

43 ... in writing?
   (A) almost always   (C) not very often
   (B) often   (D) almost never

44 How often can you tell (while listening) when a speaker breaks a rule of English you know?

   (A) almost always   (C) not very often
   (B) often   (D) almost never

45 How often can you tell (while reading) when a writer breaks a rule of English you know?

   (A) almost always   (C) not very often
   (B) often   (D) almost never

How often do you think you don't know ...

46 ... how to speak English?

   (A) almost always   (C) not very often
   (B) often   (D) almost never

47 ... correct English pronunciation?

   (A) almost always   (C) not very often
   (B) often   (D) almost never

48 ... correct English grammar?

   (A) almost always   (C) not very often
   (B) often   (D) almost never

49 ... correct English vocabulary?

   (A) almost always   (C) not very often
   (B) often   (D) almost never

50 ... how to put several English sentences together in a row?

   (A) almost always   (C) not very often
   (B) often   (D) almost never

51 ... how to use the right kind of English with different kinds of people (professors, friends, children, etc.)?

   (A) almost always   (C) not very often
   (B) often   (D) almost never

52 ... how to write English?

   (A) almost always   (C) not very often
   (B) often   (D) almost never

How often do you think you make mistakes in ...

53 ... speaking English?
  (A) almost always   (C) not very often
  (B) often   (D) almost never

54 ... English pronunciation?
  (A) almost always   (C) not very often
  (B) often   (D) almost never

55 ... English grammar?
  (A) almost always   (C) not very often
  (B) often   (D) almost never

56 ... English vocabulary?
  (A) almost always   (C) not very often
  (B) often   (D) almost never

57 ... putting several English sentences together correctly?
  (A) almost always   (C) not very often
  (B) often   (D) almost never

58 ... using the right kind of English with different kinds of people?
  (A) almost always   (C) not very often
  (B) often   (D) almost never

59 ... writing English?
  (A) almost always   (C) not very often
  (B) often   (D) almost never

In general, can you tell when someone makes a mistake in ...

60 ... speaking English?
  (A) almost always   (C) not very often
  (B) often   (D) almost never

61 ... English pronunciation?
  (A) almost always   (C) not very often
  (B) often   (D) almost never

62 ... English grammar?
   (A) almost always   (C) not very often
   (B) often   (D) almost never

63 ... English vocabulary?
   (A) almost always   (C) not very often
   (B) often   (D) almost never

64 ... putting several English sentences together correctly?
   (A) almost always   (C) not very often
   (B) often   (D) almost never

65 ... using the right kind of English with different kinds of people?
   (A) almost always   (C) not very often
   (B) often   (D) almost never

66 ... writing English?
   (A) almost always   (C) not very often
   (B) often   (D) almost never

Table of Conversion for Labels

Variable/ Factor	Label in Appendices (Pages 94 - 119)	Label in Main Study (Pages 1 - 82)
V1	HF1BQ07	BQ07
V2	HF2BQ09	BQ09
V3	HF4BQ10	BQ10
V4	HI1BQ14	BQ14
V5	HI2BQ15	BQ15
V6	HI14BQ17	BQ17
V7	ES1BQ20	BQ20
V8	ES3BQ23	BQ23
V9	ES5BQ28	BQ28
V10	MN2BQ39	BQ39
V11	MN3BQ40	BQ40
V12	MN4BQ41	BQ41
V13	FC1	FCE1
V14	FC2	FCE2
V15	FC3	FCE3
V16	TL2	TOEFL2
V17	TL3	TOEFL3
V18	TEW	TEW
V19	FC4	FCE4
V20	FC5	FCE5
V21	TL1	TOEFL1
V22	SPCOM	SPK COMP
V23	SPG	SPK GRAM
V24	SPP	SPK PRON
V25	SPF	SPK FLCY
F1	HFORM	HCF
F2	HINFORM	HCI
F3	ESCOUNT	ESC
F4, D4	MONITO	MON
F5, D5	FC123	RW1
F6, D6	TL23TEW	RW2
F7, D7	FC45TL1	LSI
F8, D8	SPCGPF	LS2

Note: The labels in the appendices that follow differ slightly from the labels in the main study. However, the variables, factors and disturbances are the same.

Appendix 2 Correlations among independent variables (disturbances) of Models 1A and 2A

Model 1A: NIE Group

		$\underline{D}$
D6	-TL23TEW	.916*
D5	-FC123	
D7	-FC45TL1	.914*
D5	-FC123	
D8	-SPCGPF	.696*
D5	-FC123	
D7	-FC45TL1	.827*
D6	-TL23TEW	
D8	-SPCGPF	.614*
D6	-TL23TEW	
D8	-SPCGPF	.715*
D7	-FC45TL1	

Model 1A: IE Group

		$\underline{D}$
D6	-TL23TEW	.828
D5	-FC123	
D7	-FC45TL1	.755*
D5	-FC123	
D8	-SPCGPF	.516*
D5	-FC123	
D7	-FC45TL1	.734*
D6	-TL23TEW	
D8	-SPCGPF	.442*
D6	-TL23TEW	
D8	-SPCGPF	.716*
D7	-FC45TL1	

Model 2A: NIE Group

D

		D
D6	-TL23TEW	.906*
D5	-FC123	
D7	-FC45TL1	.908*
D5	-FC123	
D8	-SPCGPF	.695*
D5	-FC123	
D7	-FC45TL1	.810*
D6	-TL23TEW	
D8	-SPCGPF	.611*
D6	-TL23TEW	
D8	-SPCGPF	.713*
D7	-FC45TL1	

Model 2A: IE Group

D

		D
D6	-TL23TEW	.813*
D5	-FC123	
D7	-FC45TL1	.772*
D5	-FC123	
D8	-SPCGPF	.534*
D5	-FC123	
D7	-FC45TL1	.711*
D6	-TL23TEW	
D8	-SPCGPF	.435*
D6	-TL23TEW	
D8	-SPCGPF	.735*
D7	-FC45TL1	

Appendix 3 Model 1: Figures, standardized estimates for paths and correlations among independent variables

Model 1B: IE Group

Standardized solution

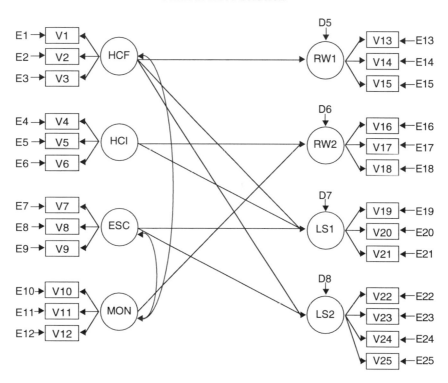

Chi-square = 793.421 based on 259 degrees of freedom
Probability value for the chi-square statistic is less than 0.001
Bentler-Bonett normed fit index = 0.878
Bentler-Bonett nonnormed fit index = 0.900
Comparative fit index = 0.914

HF1BQ07	=V1	=	.380*F1	+	.925 E1					
HF2BQ09	=V2	=	.719*F1	+	.695 E2					
HF4BQ10	=V3	=	.537 F1	+	.843 E3					
HI1BQ14	=V4	=	.515*F2	+	.857 E4					
HI2BQ15	=V5	=	.764*F2	+	.645 E5					
HI4BQ17	=V6	=	.970 F2	+	.243 E6					
ES1BQ20	=V7	=	.860*F3	+	.510 E7					
ES3BQ23	=V8	=	.711 F3	+	.703 E8					
ES5BQ28	=V9	=	.640*F3	+	.768 E9					
MN2BQ39	=V10	=	.383*F4	+	.924 E10					
MN3BQ40	=V11	=	.700*F4	+	.714 E11					
MN4BQ41	=V12	=	.775 F4	+	.633 E12					
FC1	=V13	=	.731*F5	+	.683 E13					
FC2	=V14	=	.565*F5	+	.825 E14					
FC3	=V15	=	.735 F5	+	.678 E15					
TL2	=V16	=	.866 F6	+	.500 E16					
TL3	=V17	=	.768*F6	+	.640 E17					
TEW	=V18	=	.522*F6	+	.853 E18					
FC4	−V19	=	.559 F7	+	.829 E19					
FC5	=V20	=	.593*F7	+	.805 E20					
TL1	=V21	=	.789*F7	+	.614 E21					
SPCOM	=V22	=	.994*F8	+	.110 E22					
SPG	=V23	=	.878*F8	+	.478 E23					
SPP	=V24	=	.697*F8	+	.717 E24					
SPF	=V25	=	.874 F8	+	.487 E25					
FC123	=F5	=	-.145*F1	+	.989 D5					
TL23TEW	=F6	=	.131*F2	+	.081*F4	+	.988 D6			
FC45TL1	=F7	=	-.343*F1	+	.130*F2	+	.147*F3	+	.919 D7	
SPCGPF	=F8	=	-.187*F1	+	.161*F3	+	.969 D8			

Correlations among independent variables

F				D		
F4	-MONITO	.132*				
F1	-HFORM			D6	-TL23TEW	.815*
				D5	-FC123	
F4	-MONITO	-.234*				
F3	-ESCOUNT			D7	-FC45TL1	.759*
				D5	-FC123	
				D8	-SPCGPF	.525*
				D5	-FC123	
				D7	-FC45TL1	.734*
				D6	-TL23TEW	
				D8	-SPCGPF	.443*
				D6	-TL23TEW	
				D8	-SPCGPF	.721*
				D7	-FC45TL1	

Model 1C: IE Group

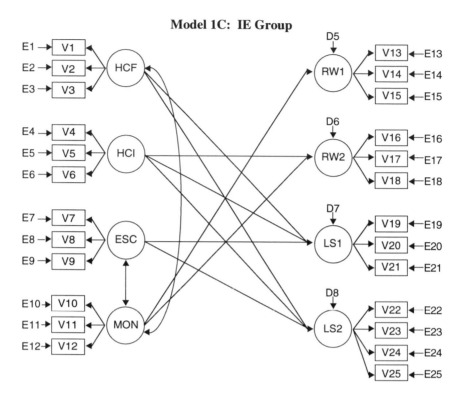

Chi-square = 798.675 based on 258 degrees of freedom
Probability value for the chi-square statistic is less than 0.001
Bentler-Bonett normed fit index = 0.877
Bentler-Bonett nonnormed fit index = 0.899
Comparative fit index = 0.913

Standardized solution

HF1BQ07	=V1	=	.443*F1	+	.896 E1					
HF2BQ09	=V2	=	.624*F1	+	.781 E2					
HF4BQ10	=V3	=	.601 F1	+	.800 E3					
HI1BQ14	=V4	=	.515*F2	+	.857 E4					
HI2BQ15	=V5	=	.763*F2	+	.646 E5					
HI4BQ17	=V6	=	.971 F2	+	.240 E6					
ES1BQ20	=V7	=	.861*F3	+	.509 E7					
ES3BQ23	=V8	=	.711 F3	+	.704 E8					
ES5BQ28	=V9	=	.639*F3	+	.769 E9					
MN2BQ39	=V10	=	.387*F4	+	.922 E10					
MN3BQ40	=V11	=	.709*F4	+	.705 E11					
MN4BQ41	=V12	=	.765 F4	+	.644 E12					
FC1	=V13	=	.723*F5	+	.691 E13					
FC2	=V14	=	.569*F5	+	.822 E14					
FC3	=V15	=	.741 F5	+	.672 E15					
TL2	=V16	=	.870 F6	+	.492 E16					
TL3	=V17	=	.765*F6	+	.644 E17					
TEW	=V18	=	.524*F6	+	.851 E18					
FC4	=V19	=	.556 F7	+	.831 E19					
FC5	=V20	=	.591*F7	+	.807 E20					
TL1	=V21	=	.785*F7	+	.620 E21					
SPCOM	=V22	=	.994*F8	+	.110 E22					
SPG	=V23	=	.878*F8	+	.479 E23					
SPP	=V24	=	.696*F8	+	.718 E24					
SPF	=V25	=	.873 F8	+	.488 E25					
FC123	=F5	=	.046*F4	+	.999 D5					
TL23TEW	=F6	=	.134*F2	+	.111*F4	+	.985 D6			
FC45TL1	=F7	=	-.273*F1	+	.135*F2	+	.143*F3	+	.942 D7	
SPCGPF	=F8	=	-.119*F1	+	.014*F2	+	.157*F3	+	.980 D8	

Correlations among independent variables

F				D		
F4	-MONITO	.159*				
F1	-HFORM			D6	-TL23TEW	.805*
				D5	-FC123	
F4	-MONITO	-.233*				
F3	-ESCOUNT			D7	-FC45TL1	.774*
				D5	-FC123	
				D8	-SPCGPF	.536*
				D5	-FC123	
				D7	-FC45TL1	.719*
				D6	-TL23TEW	
				D8	-SPCGPF	.438*
				D6	-TL23TEW	
				D8	-SPCGPF	.729*
				D7	-FC45TL1	

Appendix 4 Model 2: Figures, standardized estimates for paths and correlations among independent variables

Model 2B: NIE Group

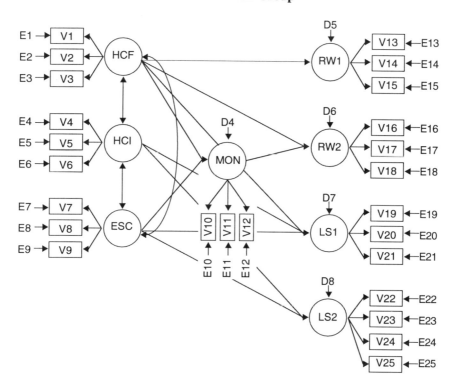

Chi-square = 574.607 based on 258 degrees of freedom
Probability value for the chi-square statistic is less than 0.001

Satorra-Bentler scaled chi-square = 576.9503
Probability value for the chi-square statistic is 0.00000

Bentler-Bonett normed fit index = 0.894
Bentler-Bonett nonnormed fit index = 0.928
Comparative fit index = 0.938

Standardized solution

HF1BQ07	=V1	=	.397*F1	+	.918 E1						
HF2BQ09	=V2	=	.748*F1	+	.664 E2						
HF4BQ10	=V3	=	.554 F1	+	.833 E3						
HI1BQ14	=V4	=	.830*F2	+	.557 E4						
HI2BQ15	=V5	=	.835*F2	+	.550 E5						
HI4BQ17	=V6	=	.920 F2	+	.393 E6						
ES1BQ20	=V7	=	.833*F3	+	.554 E7						
ES3BQ23	=V8	=	.654 F3	+	.756 E8						
ES5BQ28	=V9	=	.850*F3	+	.527 E9						
MN2BQ39	=V10	=	.383*F4	+	.924 E10						
MN3BQ40	=V11	=	.576*F4	+	.817 E11						
MN4BQ41	=V12	=	.817 F4	+	.576 E12						
FC1	=V13	=	.816*F5	+	.578 E13						
FC2	=V14	=	.770*F5	+	.638 E14						
FC3	=V15	=	.894 F5	+	.447 E15						
TL2	=V16	=	.800 F6	+	.600 E16						
TL3	=V17	=	.817*F6	+	.577 E17						
TEW	=V18	=	.681*F6	+	.732 E18						
FC4	=V19	=	.759 F7	+	.651 E19						
FC5	=V20	=	.661*F7	+	.751 E20						
TL1	=V21	=	.898*F7	+	.439 E21						
SPCOM	=V22	=	.994*F8	+	.113 E22						
SPG	=V23	=	.882*F8	+	.471 E23						
SPP	=V24	=	.704*F8	+	.711 E24						
SPF	=V25	=	.817 F8	+	.577 E25						
MONITO	=F4	=	.288*F1	+	-.161*F3	+	.933 D4				
FC123	=F5	=	.297*F1	+	.955 D5						
TL23TEW	=F6	=	.068*F4	+	.336*F1	+	.931 D6				
FC45TL1	=F7	=	.333*F1	+	.107*F2	+	.270*F3	+	.920 D7	
SPCGPF	=F8	=	.142*F2	+	.180*F3	+	.973*D8				

Correlations among independent variables

F				D		
F3	-ESCOUNT	.227*		D6	-TL23TEW	.909*
F1	-HFORM			D5	-FC123	
				D7	-FC45TL1	.902*
				D5	-FC123	
				D8	-SPCGPF	.698*
				D5	-FC123	
				D7	-FC45TL1	.810*
				D6	-TL23TEW	
				D8	-SPCGPF	.617*
				D6	-TL23TEW	
				D8	-SPCGPF	.716*
				D7	-FC45TL1	

Model 2C: NIE Group

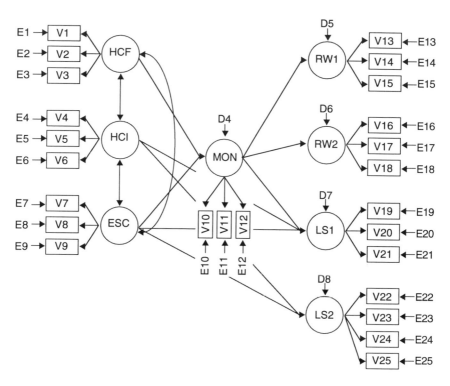

Chi-square = 576.288 based on 259 degrees of freedom
Probability value for the chi-square statistic is less than 0.001

Satorra-Bentler scaled chi-square = 577.5442
Probability value for the chi-square statistic is 0.00000

Bentler-Bonett normed fit index = 0.894
Bentler-Bonett nonnormed fit index = 0.928
Comparative fit index = 0.938

Standardized solution

HF1BQ07	=V1	=	.301*F1	+	.954 E1					
HF2BQ09	=V2	=	.994*F1	+	.110 E2					
HF4BQ10	=V3	=	.448 F1	+	.894 E3					
HI1BQ14	=V4	=	.830*F2	+	.557 E4					
HI2BQ15	=V5	=	.836*F2	+	.549 E5					
HI4BQ17	=V6	=	.919 F2	+	.394 E6					
ES1BQ20	=V7	=	.832*F3	+	.555 E7					
ES3BQ23	=V8	=	.656 F3	+	.754 E8					
ES5BQ28	=V9	=	.850*F3	+	.527 E9					
MN2BQ39	=V10	=	.404*F4	+	.915 E10					
MN3BQ40	=V11	=	.571*F4	+	.821 E11					
MN4BQ41	=V12	=	.802 F4	+	.597 E12					
FC1	=V13	=	.809*F5	+	.587 E13					
FC2	=V14	=	.762*F5	+	.648 E14					
FC3	=V15	=	.892 F5	+	.451 E15					
TL2	=V16	=	.801 F6	+	.598 E16					
TL3	=V17	=	.816*F6	+	.578 E17					
TEW	=V18	=	.674*F6	+	.739 E18					
FC4	=V19	=	.757 F7	+	.654 E19					
FC5	=V20	=	.654*F7	+	.756 E20					
TL1	=V21	=	.900*F7	+	.435 E21					
SPCOM	=V22	=	.993*F8	+	.115 E22					
SPG	=V23	=	.883*F8	+	.470 E23					
SPP	=V24	=	.703*F8	+	.711 E24					
SPF	=V25	=	.817 F8	+	.576 E25					
MONITO	=F4	=	.196*F1	+	-.157*F3	+	.960 D4			
FC123	=F5	=	.319*F4	+	.948 D5					
TL23TEW	=F6	=	.335*F4	+	.942 D6	+				
FC45TL1	=F7	=	.192*F4	+	.106*F2	+	.233*F3	+	.957 D7	
SPCGPF	=F8	=	.142*F2	+	.184*F3	+	.973 D8			

Correlations among independent variables

	F				D	
F4	-ESCOUNT	-.246*		D6	-TL23TEW	.905*
F1	-HFORM			D5	-FC123	
				D7	-FC45TL1	.906*
				D5	-FC123	
				D8	-SPCGPF	.681*
				D5	-FC123	
				D7	-FC45TL1	.816*
				D6	-TL23TEW	
				D8	-SPCGPF	.587*
				D6	-TL23TEW	
				D8	-SPCGPF	.679*
				D7	-FC45TL1	

Model 2D: NIE Group

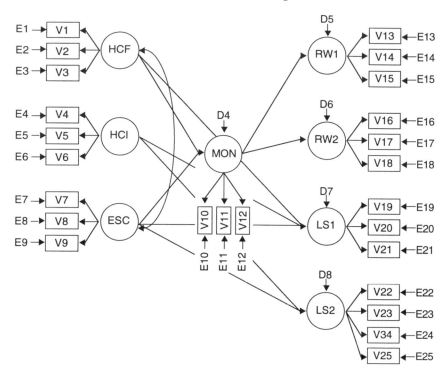

Chi-square = 578.782 based on 259 degrees of freedom
Probability value for the chi-square statistic is less than 0.001

Satorra-Bentler scaled chi-square = 581.5836
Probability value for the chi-square statistic is 0.00000

Bentler-Bonett normed fit index = 0.893
Bentler-Bonett nonnormed fit index = 0.928
Comparative fit index = 0.938

Standardized solution

HF1BQ07	=V1	=	.350*F1	+	.937 E1
HF2BQ09	=V2	=	.843*F1	+	.538 E2
HF4BQ10	=V3	=	.520 F1	+	.854 E3
HI1BQ14	=V4	=	.831*F2	+	.557 E4
HI2BQ15	=V5	=	.836*F2	+	.548 E5
HI4BQ17	=V6	=	.919 F2	+	.395 E6
ES1BQ20	=V7	=	.833*F3	+	.553 E7
ES3BQ23	=V8	=	.656 F3	+	.755 E8
ES5BQ28	=V9	=	.849*F3	+	.529 E9
MN2BQ39	=V10	=	.399*F4	+	.917 E10
MN3BQ40	=V11	=	.570*F4	+	.822 E11
MN4BQ41	=V12	=	.803 F4	+	.596 E12
FC1	=V13	=	.809*F5	+	.588 E13
FC2	=V14	=	.759*F5	+	.651 E14
FC3	=V15	=	.890 F5	+	.456 E15
TL2	=V16	=	.800 F6	+	.600 E16
TL3	=V17	=	.813*F6	+	.583 E17
TEW	=V18	=	.671*F6	+	.742 E18
FC4	=V19	=	.755 F7	+	.656 E19
FC5	=V20	=	.657*F7	+	.754 E20
TL1	=V21	=	.903*F7	+	.429 E21
SPCOM	=V22	=	.993*F8	+	.118 E22
SPG	=V23	=	.883*F8	+	.469 E23
SPP	=V24	=	.705*F8	+	.710 E24
SPF	=V25	=	.818 F8	+	.575 E25

MONITO	=F4	=	.269*F1	+	-.135*F3	+	.944 D4			
FC123	=F5	=	.231*F4	+	.973 D5					
TL23TEW	=F6	=	.256*F4	+	.967 D6					
FC45TL1	=F7	=	.152*F1	+	.105*F2	+	.247*F3	+	.962 D7
SPCGPF	=F8	=	.142*F2	+	.197*F3	+	.970 D8			

Correlations among independent variables

F				D		
F3	-ESCOUNT	-.260*		D6	-TL23TEW	.908*
F1	-HFORM			D5	-FC123	
				D7	-FC45TL1	.914*
				D5	-FC123	
				D8	-SPCGPF	.682*
				D5	-FC123	
				D7	-FC45TL1	.820*
				D6	-TL23TEW	
				D8	-SPCGPF	.591*
				D6	-TL23TEW	
				D8	-SPCGPF	.698*
				D7	-FC45TL1	

Model 2B: IE Group

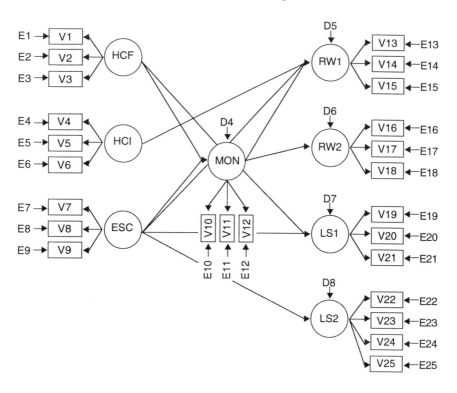

Chi-square = 788.348 based on 261 degrees of freedom
Probability value for the chi-square statistic is less than 0.001

Bentler-Bonett normed fit index = 0.879
Bentler-Bonett nonnormed fit index = 0.902
Comparative fit index = 0.915

Standardized solution

HF1BQ07	=V1	=	.463*F1	+	.886 E1				
HF2BQ09	=V2	=	.584*F1	+	.812 E2				
HF4BQ10	=V3	=	.629 F1	+	.778 E3				
HI1BQ14	=V4	=	.517*F2	+	.856 E4				
HI2BQ15	=V5	=	.765*F2	+	.643 E5				
HI4BQ17	=V6	=	.968 F2	+	.251 E6				
ES1BQ20	=V7	=	.884*F3	+	.467 E7				
ES3BQ23	=V8	=	.698 F3	+	.716 E8				
ES5BQ28	=V9	=	.620*F3	+	.785 E9				
MN2BQ39	=V10	=	.383*F4	+	.924 E10				
MN3BQ40	=V11	=	.708*F4	+	.706 E11				
MN4BQ41	=V12	=	.768 F4	+	.640 E12				
FC1	=V13	=	.737*F5	+	.676 E13				
FC2	=V14	=	.560*F5	+	.828 E14				
FC3	=V15	=	.730 F5	+	.684 E15				
TL2	=V16	=	.875 F6	+	.485 E16				
TL3	=V17	=	.756 F6	+	.655 E17				
TEW	=V18	=	.523*F6	+	.853 E18				
FC4	=V19	=	.554 F7	+	.832 E19				
FC5	=V20	=	.588*F7	+	.809 E20				
TL1	=V21	=	.786*F7	+	.619 E21				
SPCOM	=V22	=	.995*F8	+	.104 E22				
SPG	=V23	=	.879*F8	+	.477 E23				
SPP	=V24	=	.699*F8	+	.715 E24				
SPF	=V25	=	.874 F8	+	.485 E25				
MONITO	=F4	=	.168*F1	+	-.229*F3	+	.959 D4		
FC123	=F5	=	-.134*F2	+	.205*F3	+	.970 D5		
TL23TEW	=F6	=	.064*F4	+	.998 D6				
FC45TL1	=F7	=	-.214*F1	+	.223*F3	+	.951 D7		
SPCGPF	=F8	=	.220*F3	+	.976 D8				

Correlations among independent variables

	D	
D6 -TL23TEW		.814*
D5 -FC123		
D7 -FC45TL1		.767*
D5 -FC123		
D8 -SPCGPF		.530*
D5 -FC123		
D7 -FC45TL1		.709*
D6 -TL23TEW		
D8 -SPCGPF		.429*
D6 -TL23TEW		
D8 -SPCGPF		.728*
D7 -FC45TL1		

Model 2C: IE Group

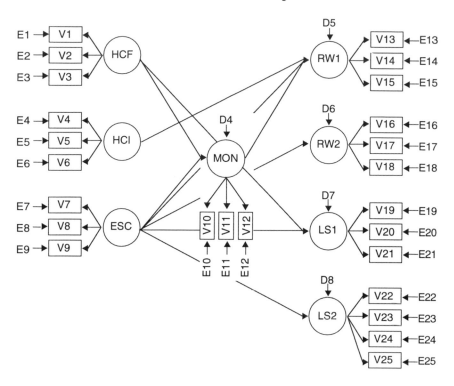

Chi-square = 789.393 based on 261 degrees of freedom
Probability value for the chi-square statistic is less than 0.001

Bentler-Bonett normed fit index = 0.879
Bentler-Bonett nonnormed fit index = 0.902
Comparative fit index = 0.915

Standardized solution

HF1BQ07	=V1	=	.464*F1	+	.886 E1			
HF2BQ09	=V2	=	.582*F1	+	.813 E2			
HF4BQ10	=V3	=	.628 F1	+	.778 E3			
HI1BQ14	=V4	=	.517*F2	+	.856 E4			
HI2BQ15	=V5	=	.765*F2	+	.644 E5			
HI4BQ17	=V6	=	.968 F2	+	.251 E6			
ES1BQ20	=V7	=	.881*F3	+	.473 E7			
ES3BQ23	=V8	=	.699 F3	+	.715 E8			
ES5BQ28	=V9	=	.623*F3	+	.782 E9			
MN2BQ39	=V10	=	.377*F4	+	.926 E10			
MN3BQ40	=V11	=	.712*F4	+	.702 E11			
MN4BQ41	=V12	=	.767 F4	+	.642 E12			
FC1	=V13	=	.736*F5	+	.677 E13			
FC2	=V14	=	.565*F5	+	.825 E14			
FC3	=V15	=	.735 F5	+	.678 E15			
TL2	=V16	=	.872 F6	+	.489 E16			
TL3	=V17	=	.760*F6	+	.650 E17			
TEW	=V18	=	.521*F6	+	.854 E18			
FC4	=V19	=	.557 F7	+	.831 E19			
FC5	=V20	=	.592*F7	+	.806 E20			
TL1	=V21	=	.788*F7	+	.616 E21			
SPCOM	=V22	=	.995*F8	+	.103 E22			
SPG	=V23	=	.880*F8	+	.475 E23			
SPP	=V24	=	.701*F8	+	.713 E24			
SPF	=V25	=	.875 F8	+	.483 E25			
MONITO	=F4	=	.169*F1	+	-.232*F3	+	.958 D4	
FC123	=F5	=	-.133*F2	+	.249*F3	+	.959 D5	
TL23TEW	=F6	=	.058*F3	+	.998 D6			
FC45TL1	=F7	=	-.216*F1	+	.261*F3	+	.941 D7	
SPCGPF	=F8	=	.243*F3	+	.970 D8			

Correlations among independent variables

	D
D6 -TL23TEW D5 -FC123	.814*
D7 -FC45TL1 D5 -FC123	.765*
D8 -SPCGPF D5 -FC123	.528*
D7 -FC45TL1 D6 -TL23TEW	.703*
D8 -SPCGPF D6 -TL23TEW	.425*
D8 -SPCGPF D7 -FC45TL1	.727*

Model 2D: IE Group

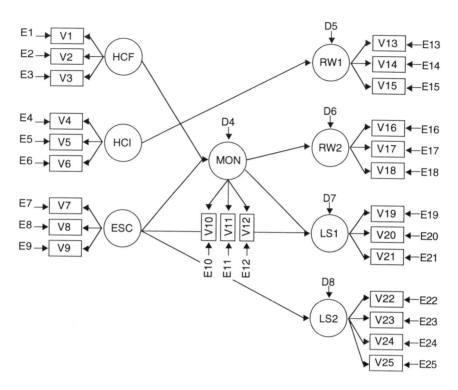

Chi-square = 811.822 based on 262 degrees of freedom
Probability value for the chi-square statistic is less than 0.001

Bentler-Bonett normed fit index = 0.875
Bentler-Bonett nonnormed fit index = 0.898
Comparative fit index = 0.911

Standardized solution

HF1BQ07	=V1	=	.461*F1	+	.887 E1				
HF2BQ09	=V2	=	.585*F1	+	.811 E2				
HF4BQ10	=V3	=	.629 F1	+	.778 E3				
HI1BQ14	=V4	=	.515*F2	+	.857 E4				
HI2BQ15	=V5	=	.762*F2	+	.647 E5				
HI4BQ17	=V6	=	.972 F2	+	.234 E6				
ES1BQ20	=V7	=	.860*F3	+	.510 E7				
ES3BQ23	=V8	=	.711 F3	+	.703 E8				
ES5BQ28	=V9	=	.639*F3	+	.769 E9				
MN2BQ39	=V10	=	.386*F4	+	.923 E10				
MN3BQ40	=V11	=	.705*F4	+	.709 E11				
MN4BQ41	=V12	=	.769 F4	+	.640 E12				
FC1	=V13	=	.731*F5	+	.682 E13				
FC2	=V14	=	.568*F5	+	.823 E14				
FC3	=V15	=	.739 F5	+	.673 E15				
TL2	=V16	=	.871 F6	+	.491 E16				
TL3	=V17	=	.762*F6	+	.648 E17				
TEW	=V18	=	.520*F6	+	.854 E18				
FC4	=V19	=	.552 F7	+	.834 E19				
FC5	=V20	=	.585*F7	+	.811 E20				
TL1	=V21	=	.784*F7	+	.621 E21				
SPCOM	=V22	=	.995*F8	+	.105 E22				
SPG	=V23	=	.878*F8	+	.479 E23				
SPP	=V24	=	.697*F8	+	.717 E24				
SPF	=V25	=	.873 F8	+	.487 E25				
MONITO	=F4	=	.168*F1	+	-.240*F3	+	.956 D4		
FC123	=F5	=	-.138*F2	+	.990 D5				
TL23TEW	=F6	=	.094*F4	+	.996 D6				
FC45TL1	=F7	=	-.213*F1	+	.143*F3	+	.967 D7		
SPCGPF	=F8	=	.154*F3	+	.988 D8				

Correlations among independent variables

		D
D6 -TL23TEW		.805*
D5 -FC123		
D7 -FC45TL1		.769*
D5 -FC123		
D8 -SPCGPF		.537*
D5 -FC123		
D7 -FC45TL1		.710*
D6 -TL23TEW		
D8 -SPCGPF		.431*
D6 -TL23TEW		
D8 -SPCGPF		.732*
D7 -FC45TL1		

Appendix 5: EQS Computer programing for selected models

(Only for the NIE group; modifications will be necessary for the IE group in terms of the following: DATA DD DSN, TITLE, CASES and DELETE.)

Model for TTCs

```
1  //IYG9LFB JOB,TIME=(7,0)
2  // EXEC EQS,RG=6144K,SIZE=900000
3  //DATA DD DSN=IYG9LFB.JAN31.DATA.GRP1,DISP=SHR
4  /TITLE ANTONY KUNNAN; Oct 18, 1991;
5  FILE EQS.MODEL14.GRP1.4FACT
6  CAMB DATA EQS; MODEL 14: F1 TO F4 (TTCs 4 FACTOR UNCORR MODEL)
7  /SPECIFICATIONS
   CASES=380; VARIABLES=12; METHOD=ML,ROBUST; MATRIX=RAW;
8  DELETE=55,61,163,168,97,145,143,96,50,95,148,132,110,5,108,144, 92,107,142,167;
9  FO='(18x,1f1,1x,2f1,3x,2f1,1x,1f1,2x,1f1,2x,1f1,4x,1f1,1x,9x,3f1,64x)';
/LABELS
   V1=HF1BQ07;      V2=HF2BQ09;      V3=HF4BQ10;
   V4=HI1BQ14;      V5=HI2BQ15;      V6=HI4BQ17;
   V7=ES1BQ20;      V8=ES3BQ23;      V9=ES5BQ28;
   V10=MN2BQ39;     V11=MN3BQ40;     V12=MN4BQ41;
   F1=HFORM;        F2=HINFORM;      F3=ESCOUNT;      F4=MONITOR;
/EQUATIONS
        V1  =      1*F1          +    E1;
        V2  =      1*F1          +    E2;
        V3  =      1F1           +    E3;
        V4  =      1*F2          +    E4;
        V5  =      1*F2          +    E5;
        V6  =      1F2           +    E6;
        V7  =      1*F3          +    E7;
        V8  =      1F3           +    E8;
        V9  =      2*F3          +    E9;
        V10 =      1*F4          +    E10;
        V11 =      2*F4          +    E11;
        V12 =      1F4           +    E12;
/VARIANCES
    F1 TO F4 = 10*;
    E1 TO E9 = 60*;
    E10 TO E12 = 50*;
/COVARIANCES
    F1,F3 = .3*;
    F3,F4 = .3*;
    F1,F4 = .2*;
```

```
/TECHNICAL
   ITR=100;
/PRINT
   EFFECT=YES;
   COR=YES;
/LMTEST
/WTEST
/END
```

Model: TP factors - Higher-order factors

Modify lines 1 to 9 as required

```
/LABELS
   V1=FC1;        V2=FC2;        V3=FC3;        V4=TL2;        V5=TL3;
   V6=TEW;        V7=FC4;        V8=FC5;        V9=TL1;        V10=SPCOM;
   V11=SPG;       V12=SPP;       V13=SPF;
   F1=GFACTOR;    F2=FC123;      F3=TL23TEW;    F4=FC45TL1;    F5=SPCGPF;
   /EQUATIONS
   V1   =         1*F2           +   E1;
   V2   =         1*F2           +   E2;
   V3   =         1F2            +   E3;
   V4   =         1*F3           +   E4;
   V5   =         1F3            +   E5;
   V6   =         1*F3           +   E6;
   V7   =         1*F4           +   E7;
   V8   =         1*F4           +   E8;
   V9   =         1F4            +   E9;
   V10  =         1*F5           +   E10;
   V11  =         1*F5           +   E11;
   V12  =         1*F5           +   E12;
   V13  =         1F5            +   E13;
   F2   =         1*F1           +   D2;
   F3   =         1*F1           +   D3;
   F4   =         1*F1           +   D4;
   F5   =         1*F1           +   D5;
/VARIANCES
   F1 = 1;
   E1 TO E9 = 80*;
   E10 TO E13 = 60*;
/CONSTRAINTS
   (F2,F1) = (F3,F1);
   (F2,F1) = (F4,F1);
   (F2,F1) = (F5,F1);
/TECHNICAL
   ITR=100;
/PRINT
   EFFECT=YES;
   COR=YES;
/LMTEST
/WTEST
/END
```

Model: TP factors - Nested factors

Modify lines 1 to 9 as required

```
/LABELS
    V1=FC1;         V2=FC2;       V3=FC3;         V4=TL2;        V5=TL3;
    V6=TEW;         V7=FC4;       V8=FC5;         V9=TL1;        V10=SPCOM;
    V11=SPG;        V12=SPP;      V13=SPF;
    F1=GFACTOR;     F2=FC123;     F3=TL23TEW;     F4=FC45TL1;    F5=SPCGPF;
/EQUATIONS
    V1   =          1*F1    +    1F2    +    E1;
    V2   =          1*F1    +    1F2    +    E2;
    V3   =          1*F1    +    1F2    +    E3;
    V4   =          1*F1    +    1F3    +    E4;
    V5   =          1*F1    +    1F3    +    E5;
    V6   =          1*F1    +    1F3    +    E6;
    V7   =          1*F1    +    1F4    +    E7;
    V8   =          1*F1    +    1F4    +    E8;
    V9   =          1*F1    +    1F4    +    E9;
    V10  =          1*F1    +    1F5    +    E10;
    V11  =          1*F1    +    1F5    +    E11;
    V12  =          1*F1    +    1F5    +    E12;
    V13  =          1*F1    +    1F5    +    E13;
/VARIANCES
    F2 TO F5 = 1;
    E1 TO E9 = 80*;
    E10 TO E13 = 60*;
/CONSTRAINTS
    (V1,F1) = (V2,F1);
    (V1,F1) = (V3,F1);
    (V1,F1) = (V4,F1);
    (V1,F1) = (V5,F1);
    (V1,F1) = (V6,F1);
    (V1,F1) = (V7,F1);
    (V1,F1) = (V8,F1);
    (V1,F1) = (V9,F1);
    (V1,F1) = (V10,F1);
    (V1,F1) = (V11,F1);
    (V1,F1) = (V12,F1);
    (V1,F1) = (V13,F1);
/TECHNICAL
    ITR=100;
/PRINT
    EFFECT=YES;
    COR=YES;
/LMTEST
/WTEST
/END
```

Model: TP factors - Correlated factors

Modify lines 1 to 9 as required

```
/LABELS
    V1=FC1;         V2=FC2;         V3=FC3;         V4=TL2;     V5=TL3;
    V6=TEW;         V7=FC4;         V8=FC5;         V9=TL1;     V10=SPCOM;
    V11=SPG;        V12=SPP;        V13=SPF;
    F1=FC123;       F2=TL23TEW;     F3=FC45TL1;     F4=SPCGPF;
/EQUATIONS
    V1   =          1*F1            +   E1;
    V2   =          1*F1            +   E2;
    V3   =          1F1             +   E3;
    V4   =          1*F2            +   E4;
    V5   =          1F2             +   E5;
    V6   =          1*F2            +   E6;
    V7   =          1*F3            +   E7;
    V8   =          1*F3            +   E8;
    V9   =          1F3             +   E9;
    V10  =          1*F4            +   E10;
    V11  =          1*F4            +   E11;
    V12  =          1*F4            +   E12;
    V13  =          1F4             +   E13;
/VARIANCES
    F1 TO F4 = 10*;
    E1 TO E9 = 120*;
    E10 TO E13 = 110*;
/COVARIANCES
    F1,F2 =  .3*;
    F1,F3 =  .4*;
    F1,F4 =  .3*;
    F2,F3 =  .3*;
    F2,F4 =  .4*;
    F3,F4 =  .3*;
/TECHNICAL
    ITR=100;
/PRINT
    EFFECT=YES;
    COR=YES;
/LMTEST
/WTEST
/END
```

Model: TTCs and TP factors - MODEL 1A

Modify lines 1 to 9 as required

```
/LABELS
    V1=HF1BQ07;     V2=HF2BQ09;     V3=HF4BQ10;     V4=HI1BQ14;
    V5=HI2BQ15;     V6=HI4BQ17;     V7=ES1BQ20;     V8=ES3BQ23;
    V9=ES5BQ28;     V10=MN2BQ39;    V11=MN3BQ40;    V12=MN4BQ41;
    V13=FC1;        V14=FC2;        V15=FC3;        V16=TL2;
    V17=TL3;        V18=TEW;        V19=FC4;        V20=FC5;
    V21=TL1;        V22=SPCOM;      V23=SPG;        V24=SPP;
    V25=SPF;
    F1=HFORM;       F2=HINFORM;     F3=ESCOUNT;     F4=MONITO;
    F5=FC123;       F6=TL23TEW;     F7=FC45TL1;     F8=SPCGPF;
```

```
/EQUATIONS
    V1   =              1*F1              +    E1;
    V2   =              2*F1              +    E2;
    V3   =              1F1               +    E3;
    V4   =              2*F2              +    E4;
    V5   =              1*F2              +    E5;
    V6   =              1F2               +    E6;
    V7   =              1*F3              +    E7;
    V8   =              1F3               +    E8;
    V9   =              2*F3              +    E9;
    V10  =              1*F4              +    E10;
    V11  =              2*F4              +    E11;
    V12  =              1F4               +    E12;
    V13  =              1*F5              +    E13;
    V14  =              2*F5              +    E14;
    V15  =              1F5               +    E15;
    V16  =              1F6               +    E16;
    V17  =              2*F6              +    E17;
    V18  =              1*F6              +    E18;
    V19  =              1F7               +    E19;
    V20  =              2*F7              +    E20;
    V21  =              1*F7              +    E21;
    V22  =              1*F8              +    E22;
    V23  =              2*F8              +    E23;
    V24  =              1*F8              +    E24;
    V25  =              1F8               +    E25;
    F5   =    1*F4                        +    D5;
    F6   =    1*F2    +    1*F4           +    D6;
    F7   =    1*F1    +    1*F2    +    1*F3    +    D7;
    F8   =    1*F1    +    1*F2    +    1*F3    +    D8;
    /VARIANCES
    F1 TO F4 = 1*;
    E1 TO E9 = 60*;
    E10 TO E12 = 40*;
    E13 TO E18 = 20*;
    E19 TO E25 = 20*;
    D5 TO D8  = 50*;
/COVARIANCES
    F4,F3 = .3*;
    F4,F1 = .4*;
    D5,D6 = .3*;
    D6,D7 = .2*;
    D7,D8 = .3*;
    D5,D7 = .5*;
    D5,D8 = .3*;
    D6,D8 = .5*;
/TECHNICAL
    ITR=100;
/PRINT
/LMTEST
/WTEST
/END
```

Model: TTCs and TP factors - MODEL 2A

Modify lines 1 to 9 as required

```
/LABELS
V1=HF1BQ07;      V2=HF2BQ09;      V3=HF4BQ10;      V4=HI1BQ14;
V5=HI2BQ15;      V6=HI4BQ17;      V7=ES1BQ20;      V8=ES3BQ23;
V9=ES5BQ28;      V10=MN2BQ39;     V11=MN3BQ40;     V12=MN4BQ41;
V13=FC1;         V14=FC2;         V15=FC3;         V16=TL2;
V17=TL3;         V18=TEW;         V19=FC4;         V20=FC5;
V21=TL1;         V22=SPCOM;       V23=SPG;         V24=SPP;
V25=SPF;
F1=HFORM;        F2=HINFORM;      F3=ESCOUNT;      F4=MONITO;
F5=FC123;        F6=TL23TEW;      F7=FC45TL1;      F8=SPCGPF;
/EQUATIONS
    V1  =              1*F1            +    E1;
    V2  =              2*F1            +    E2;
    V3  =              1F1             +    E3;
    V4  =              2*F2            +    E4;
    V5  =              1*F2            +    E5;
    V6  =              1F2             +    E6;
    V7  =              1*F3            +    E7;
    V8  =              1F3             +    E8;
    V9  =              2*F3            +    E9;
    V10 =              1*F4            +    E10;
    V11 =              2*F4            +    E11;
    V12 =              1F4             +    E12;
    V13 =              1*F5            +    E13;
    V14 =              2*F5            +    E14;
    V15 =              1F5             +    E15;
    V16 =              1F6             +    E16;
    V17 =              2*F6            +    E17;
    V18 =              1*F6            +    E18;
    V19 =              1F7             +    E19;
    V20 =              2*F7            +    E20;
    V21 =              1*F7            +    E21;
    V22 =              1*F8            +    E22;
    V23 =              2*F8            +    E23;
    V24 =              1*F8            +    E24;
    V25 =              1F8             +    E25;
    F4  =   1*F1  +   1*F3            +    D4;
    F5  =   1*F1  +   1*F4            +    D5;
    F6  =   1*F1  +   1*F4            +    D6;
    F7  =   1*F1  +   1*F2  +   1*F3  +    D7;
    F8  =   1*F2. +   1*F3            +    D8;
/VARIANCES
    F1 TO F3 = 10*;
    E1 TO E9 = 80*;
    E10 TO E12 = 60*;
    E13 TO E18 = 40*;
    E19 TO E25 = 40*;
    D4 TO D8  = 100*;
```

```
/COVARIANCES
    F1,F3 = .3*;
    D5,D6 = .3*;
    D6,D7 = .2*;
    D7,D8 = .3*;
    D5,D8 = .5*;
    D6,D8 = .3*;
    D5,D7 = .5*;
/TECHNICAL
    ITR=100;
/PRINT
    EFFECT=YES;
    COR=YES;
/LMTEST
/WTEST
/END
```

Model: TTCs and TP factors - Nested factor MODEL

Modify lines 1 to 9 as required

```
/LABELS
V1=HF1BQ07;       V2=HF2BQ09;       V3=HF4BQ10;       V4=HI1BQ14;
V5=HI2BQ15;       V6=HI4BQ17;       V7=ES1BQ20;       V8=ES3BQ23;
V9=ES5BQ28;       V10=MN2BQ39;      V11=MN3BQ40;      V12=MN4BQ41;
V13=FC1;          V14=FC2;          V15=FC3;          V16=TL2;
V17=TL3;          V18=TEW;          V19=FC4;          V20=FC5;
V21=TL1;          V22=SPCOM;        V23=SPG;          V24=SPP;
V25=SPF;
F1=HFORM;         F2=HINFORM;       F3=ESCOUNT;       F4=MONITO;
F5=GFACTOR;       F6=FC123;         F7=TL23TEW;       F8=FC45TL1
F9=SPCGPF;
/EQUATIONS
    V1   =                 1*F1        +    E1;
    V2   =                 1*F1        +    E2;
    V3   =                 1F1         +    E3;
    V4   =                 1*F2        +    E4;
    V5   =                 1*F2        +    E5;
    V6   =                 1F2         +    E6;
    V7   =                 1*F3        +    E7;
    V8   =                 1F3         +    E8;
    V9   =                 2*F3        +    E9;
    V10  =                 1*F4        +    E10;
    V11  =                 2*F4        +    E11;
    V12  =                 1F4         +    E12;
    V13  =  1*F5    +    1F6        +    E13;
    V14  =  1*F5    +    1F6        +    E14;
    V15  =  1*F5    +    1F6        +    E15;
    V16  =  1*F5    +    1F7        +    E16;
    V17  =  1*F5    +    1F7        +    E17;
    V18  =  1*F5    +    1F7        +    E18;
    V19  =  1*F5    +    1F8        +    E19;
    V20  =  1*F5    +    1F8        +    E20;
```

```
V21  =   1*F5   +   1F8               +   E21,
V22  =   1*F5   +   1F9               +   E22;
V23  =   1*F5   +   1F9               +   E23;
V24  =   1*F5   +   1F9               +   E24;
V25  =   1*F5   +   1F9               +   E25;
F4   =   1*F1   +   1*F3              +   D4;
F6   =   1*F1   +   1*F4              +   D6;
F7   =   1*F1   +   1*F4              +   D7;
F8   =   1*F1   +   1*F2   +   1*F3   +   D8;
F9   =   1*F2   +   1*F3              +   D9;
/VARIANCES
   F1 TO F3 = 10*;
   F5 = 1;
   E1 TO E9 = 80*;
   E10 TO E12 = 60*;
   E13 TO E18 = 40*;
   E19 TO E25 = 40*;
   D4 = 100*;
   D6 TO D9 = 80*;
/COVARIANCES
   F1,F3 = .3*;
/TECHNICAL
   ITR=100;
/PRINT
   EFFECT=YES;
   COR=YES;
/LMTEST
/WTEST
/END
```

Appendix 6 Correlation matrices for TTCs, TP, and TTCs and TP together for the NIE and IE groups

NIE group correlation matrix

	BQ07	BQ09	BQ10	BQ14	BQ15	BQ17	BQ20	BQ23	BQ28	BQ39	BQ40	BQ41
BQ07	1.00000											
BQ09	.28483	1.00000										
BQ10	.17098	.43597	1.00000									
BQ14	.05655	.00030	.01548	1.00000								
BQ15	-.03257	-.04482	-.09828	.65678	1.00000							
BQ17	.03038	-.01779	-.04040	.75109	.73641	1.00000						
BQ20	-.06812	-.19465	-.04503	.09148	.08037	.03765	1.00000					
BQ23	-.02991	-.23203	.01837	-.02744	-.03447	-.05879	.55147	1.00000				
BQ28	-.01397	-.17618	-.05180	.13538	.13843	.12649	.69818	.55010	1.00000			
BQ39	.10697	.01786	.04019	.06925	.03541	.06715	-.04730	-.03452	-.05477	1.00000		
BQ40	.10090	.09412	.09885	-.00870	.02477	.01965	-.05946	-.04680	-.11276	.23915	1.00000	
BQ41	.11489	.13974	.13653	-.07160	-.00974	-.04940	-.17617	-.16219	-.14805	.31538	.47140	1.00000

IE group correlation matrix

	BQ07	BQ09	BQ10	BQ14	BQ15	BQ17	BQ20	BQ23	BQ28	BQ39	BQ40	BQ41
BQ07	1.00000											
BQ09	.23529	1.00000										
BQ10	.30044	.37901	1.00000									
BQ14	.01822	.03249	.04780	1.00000								
BQ15	-.20033	.00802	-.00145	.39308	1.00000							
BQ17	-.13300	.09664	.03356	.52859	.71720	1.00000						
BQ20	.20615	-.00866	.00837	.07137	-.00960	-.07977	1.00000					
BQ23	.07651	.00278	-.01917	.02031	.01262	-.04295	.61410	1.00000				
BQ28	.05692	.13064	.03234	.09862	.12352	.11445	.54257	.47397	1.00000			
BQ39	.11588	.14771	.05732	-.01201	-.00658	.05395	-.11552	-.05629	-.01042	1.00000		
BQ40	.10061	.03459	.09269	-.00465	-.02570	-.02024	-.10316	-.08103	-.09858	.27368	1.00000	
BQ41	-.0024	.04261	.08215	-.02286	-.03420	-.02485	-.16278	-.15198	-.11271	.28991	.55074	1.00000

NIE group correlation matrix

	FCE1	FCE2	FCE3	TOEFL2	TOEFL3	TEW	FCE4	FCE5	TOEFL1	SPK COMP	SPK GRAM	SPK PRON	SPK FLCY
FCE1	1.00000												
FCE2	.58581	1.00000											
FCE3	.72782	.68797	1.00000										
TFL2	.57468	.55307	.64962	1.00000									
TFL3	.66382	.49745	.64069	.70186	1.00000								
TEW	.49374	.57664	.61872	.52167	.49758	1.00000							
FCE4	.53744	.58092	.61043	.37745	.46895	.46596	1.00000						
FCE5	.39402	.42916	.48165	.40767	.39432	.30301	.51480	1.00000					
TFL1	.66383	.63013	.70287	.54389	.63025	.45365	.69097	.60126	1.00000				
SPCOMP	.49699	.54519	.56763	.44783	.40318	.40134	.53650	.51219	.62154	1.00000			
SPG	.40274	.49198	.49887	.40366	.32716	.35818	.46455	.45440	.54425	.87955	1.00000		
SPP	.46020	.49811	.54732	.39081	.36731	.39046	.47769	.41057	.55074	.70224	.58140	1.00000	
SPF	.50477	.51290	.56946	.41527	.37782	.44474	.53639	.51586	.59200	.81744	.68765	.64879	1.00000

IE group correlation matrix

	FCE1	FCE2	FCE3	TOEFL2	TOEFL3	TEW	FCE4	FCE5	TOEFL1	SPK COMP	SPK GRAM	SPK PRON	SPK FLCY
FCE1	1.00000												
FCE2	.39631	1.00000											
FCE3	.52794	.46772	1.00000										
TFL2	.47028	.37205	.52562	1.00000									
TFL3	.48427	.29243	.45175	.66029	1.00000								
TEW	.26666	.24844	.28990	.45930	.34540	1.00000							
FCE4	.36720	.20114	.32598	.35152	.31426	.21493	1.00000						
FCE5	.33989	.31295	.28830	.30318	.25522	.27556	.31936	1.00000					
TFL1	.48407	.31882	.38995	.45839	.38964	.33619	.48746	.43567	1.00000				
SPCOMP	.41868	.38775	.34588	.36457	.28724	.28098	.35834	.49720	.57152	1.00000			
SPG	.38743	.37630	.30824	.32733	.23937	.25966	.34581	.48696	.52070	.87893	1.00000		
SPP	.36705	.38861	.41367	.35455	.31342	.24264	.32602	.39390	.50190	.70211	.59218	1.00000	
SPF	.34131	.30821	.29348	.28413	.21533	.23322	.34233	.46349	.54079	.87086	.78312	.55513	1.00000

NIE group correlation matrix

	BQ07	BQ09	BQ10	BQ14	BQ15	BQ17	BQ20	BQ23	BQ28	BQ39	BQ40	BQ41
BQ07	1.00000											
BQ09	.28483	1.00000										
BQ10	.17098	.43597	1.00000									
BQ14	.05655	.00030	.01548	1.00000								
BQ15	-.03257	-.04482	-.09828	.65678	1.00000							
BQ17	.03038	-.01779	-.04040	.75109	.73641	1.00000						
BQ20	-.06812	-.19465	-.04503	.09148	.08037	.03765	1.00000					
BQ23	-.02991	-.23203	.01837	-.02744	-.03447	-.05879	.55147	1.00000				
BQ28	-.01397	-.17618	-.05180	.13538	.13843	.12649	.69818	.55010	1.00000			
BQ39	.10697	.01786	.04019	.06925	.03541	.06715	-.04730	-.03452	-.05477	1.00000		
BQ40	.10090	.09412	.09885	-.00870	.02477	.01965	-.05946	-.04680	-.11276	.23915	1.00000	
BQ41	.11489	.13974	.13653	-.07160	-.00974	-.04940	-.17617	-.16219	-.14805	.31538	.47140	1.00000
FCE1	.21680	.09960	.16741	-.02242	-.06977	-.02548	.04673	.05401	.00972	.24766	.12493	.28101
FCE2	.22815	.08090	.18997	.02954	-.03415	.04211	.03472	.01113	-.02303	.28550	.07175	.24902
FCE3	.26062	.19233	.16085	.10168	.04333	.09479	.04049	.03310	-.02172	.32588	.15690	.29302
TFL2	.22055	.13222	.16311	-.04473	-.09617	-.07830	.02552	.02489	-.01210	.29637	.19802	.32720
TFL3	.29876	.17281	.16504	-.04426	-.09751	-.12081	.03051	.04114	-.01993	.18790	.09823	.21751
TEW	.21789	.19028	.19943	.04780	-.09199	.00331	-.09503	-.05841	-.14485	.28031	.12656	.26870
FCE4	.22765	.08994	.16857	.12734	.01936	.11778	.13451	.11236	.12585	.23680	.10694	.16106
FCE5	.20187	.09659	.15082	.16902	.07432	.15750	.28676	.20665	.26520	.16877	.04420	.12853
TFL1	.24890	.12060	.18881	.12841	.04642	.13137	.21449	.16200	.19522	.20526	.05701	.14260
SPCOMP	.10218	-.04497	.01989	.13170	.10458	.17521	.21214	.16874	.20235	.23561	.02017	.12757
SPG	.07268	-.07666	.01290	.12064	.07010	.14727	.26635	.23224	.23499	.20708	.02419	.06252
SPP	.10652	-.05146	-.00220	.05648	.07349	.13176	.12841	.07802	.13657	.22178	.03933	.14673
SPF	.15851	.07869	.10505	.13224	.10941	.20399	.15454	.10118	.12627	.20136	.00937	.13877

NIE group correlation matrix (cont.)

	FCE1	FCE2	FCE3	TOEFL2	TOEFL3	TEW	FCE4	FCE5	TOEFL1	SPK COMP	SPK GRAM	SPK PRON	SPK FLCY
FCE1	1.00000												
FCE2	.58581	1.00000											
FCE3	.72782	.68797	1.00000										
TFL2	.57468	.55307	.64962	1.00000									
TFL3	.66382	.49745	.64069	.70186	1.00000								
TEW	.49374	.57664	.61872	.52167	.49758	1.00000							
FCE4	.53744	.58092	.61043	.37745	.46895	.46596	1.00000						
FCE5	.39402	.42916	.48165	.40767	.39432	.30301	.51480	1.00000					
TFL1	.66383	.63013	.70287	.54389	.63025	.45365	.69097	.60126	1.00000				
SPCOMP	.49699	.54519	.56763	.44783	.40318	.40134	.53650	.51219	.62154	1.00000			
SPG	.40274	.49198	.49887	.40366	.32716	.35818	.46455	.45440	.54425	.87955	1.00000		
SPP	.46020	.49811	.54732	.39081	.36731	.39046	.47769	.41057	.55074	.70224	.58140	1.00000	
SPF	.50477	.51290	.56946	.41527	.37782	.44474	.53639	.51586	.59200	.81744	.68765	.64879	1.00000

IE group correlation matrix

	BQ07	BQ09	BQ10	BQ14	BQ15	BQ17	BQ20	BQ23	BQ28	BQ39	BQ40	BQ41
BQ07	1.00000											
BQ09	.23529	1.00000										
BQ10	.30044	.37901	1.00000									
BQ14	.01822	.03249	.04780	1.00000								
BQ15	-.20033	.00802	-.00145	.39308	1.00000							
BQ17	-.13300	.09664	.03356	.52859	.71720	1.00000						
BQ20	.20615	-.00866	.00837	.07137	-.00960	-.07977	1.00000					
BQ23	.07651	.00278	-.01917	.02031	.01262	-.04295	.61410	1.00000				
BQ28	.05692	.13064	.03234	.09862	.12352	.11445	.54257	.47397	1.00000			
BQ39	.11588	.14771	.05732	-.01201	-.00658	.05395	-.11552	-.05629	-.01042	1.00000		
BQ40	.10061	.03459	.09269	-.00465	-.02570	-.02024	-.10316	-.08103	-.09858	.27368	1.00000	
BQ41	-.00244	.04261	.08215	-.02286	-.03420	-.02485	-.16278	-.15198	-.11271	.28991	.55074	1.0000C
FCE1	.04675	-.14258	-.06935	.02155	-.01863	-.03782	.21293	.16184	.09409	.02458	-.09816	-.08631
FCE2	.05956	-.06241	-.02326	.03976	.00802	.04702	.11438	.06438	.05965	.06155	.03928	.05142
FCE3	.01583	-.08685	-.04332	.01265	-.07754	-.06989	.15040	.10475	.05563	.09944	.11310	.07679
TFL2	-.07352	.03713	-.03714	-.02713	.03294	.05126	.00794	-.02362	.12088	.20787	.03494	.06108
TFL3	-.08919	.10252	.02794	.00536	.05420	.06801	.09255	.09221	.21102	.11887	-.02444	.02012
TEW	-.10325	-.01144	-.01120	.03596	.09486	.09461	-.05140	-.06693	.04674	.08019	.02387	.09725
FCE4	.01666	-.08504	-.01558	.07072	.07701	.08214	.19797	.08220	.11678	-.04048	-.10387	-.09406
FCE5	-.10170	-.13804	-.10857	.04311	.08778	.08623	.19346	.11875	.17134	-.09706	-.04694	-.01811
TFL1	-.07749	-.24457	-.12877	.09041	.07721	.05297	.15174	-.00006	.05234	-.04777	-.09228	-.05009
SPCOMP	.02425	-.17699	-.06672	.06465	.01511	.00315	.23045	.12231	.07571	-.03498	-.06616	-.02376
SPG	.02128	-.20570	-.08093	.05613	.01141	.00061	.22635	.12768	.07753	-.08685	-.09891	-.07763
SPP	.02781	-.09337	.00343	-.01873	-.00164	-.02643	.22998	.12901	.08395	.01685	-.02365	.02517
SPF	.02767	-.20418	-.04888	.07516	.02722	.03001	.18227	.07059	.02730	-.01302	-.03812	-.03393

IE group correlation matrix

	FCE1	FCE2	FCE3	TOEFL2	TOEFL3	TEW	FCE4	FCE5	TOEFL1	SPK COMP	SPK GRAM	SPK PRON	SPK FLCY
FCE1	1.00000												
FCE2	.39631	1.00000											
FCE3	.52794	.46772	1.00000										
TFL2	.47028	.37205	.52562	1.00000									
TFL3	.48427	.29243	.45175	.66029	1.00000								
TEW	.26666	.24844	.28990	.45930	.34540	1.00000							
FCE4	.36720	.20114	.32598	.35152	.31426	.21496	1.00000						
FCE5	.33989	.31295	.28830	.30318	.25522	.27556	.31936	1.00000					
TFL1	.48407	.31882	.38995	.45839	.38964	.33619	.48746	.43567	1.00000				
SPCOMP	.41868	.38775	.34588	.36457	.28724	.28098	.35834	.49720	.57152	1.00000			
SPG	.38743	.37630	.30824	.32733	.23937	.25966	.34581	.48696	.52070	.87893	1.00000		
SPP	.36705	.38861	.41367	.35455	.31342	.24264	.32602	.39390	.50190	.70211	.59218	1.00000	
SPF	.34131	.30821	.29348	.28413	.21533	.23322	.34233	.46349	.54079	.87086	.78312	.55513	1.00000

References

American Psychological Association Committee on Psychological Tests. 1954. Technical recommendations for psychological tests and diagnostic techniques. *Psychological Bulletin* 51 (2, Pt.2).

Ayer, A. J. 1936. *Language, truth, and logic.* (2nd Edn.) New York: Dover Publications.

Bachman, L. F. 1982. The trait structure of cloze test scores. *TESOL Quarterly* 16: 61–70.

Bachman, L. F. 1988. Language Testing–SLA research interfaces. *Annual Review of Applied Linguistics* 9: 193–209.

Bachman, L. F. 1990. *Fundamental considerations in language testing.* Oxford: Oxford University Press.

Bachman, L. F., F. G. Davidson and J. Foulkes. 1990. A comparison of the abilities measured by the Cambridge and Educational Testing Service EFL test batteries. *Issues in Applied Linguistics* 1, 30–55.

Bachman, L. F., F. G. Davidson and B. Lynch. 1988a. *Test method: The context for performance on language tests.* Paper presented at the 1988 Annual Meeting of the American Association for Applied Linguistics, New Orleans.

Bachman, L. F., F. G. Davidson, B. Lynch and K. Ryan. 1989. *Content analysis and statistical modeling of EFL proficiency tests.* Paper presented at the 11th Annual Language Testing Research Colloquium, San Antonio, Texas.

Bachman, L. F., F. G. Davidson and M. Milanovic. 1991. *The use of test method characteristics in the content analysis and design of EFL proficiency tests.* Paper presented at the 13th Language Testing Research Colloquium. Princeton: Educational Testing Service.

Bachman, L. F., F. G. Davidson, K. Ryan and I-C Choi. 1995. *An investigation into the comparability of two tests of English as a foreign language: The Cambridge–TOEFL comparability study.* Cambridge: UCLES.

Bachman, L. F., A. J. Kunnan, S. Vanniarajan and B. Lynch. 1988b. Task and ability analysis as a basis for examining content and construct comparability in two EFL proficiency test batteries. *Language Testing* 5(2): 128–59.

Bachman, L. F. and M. Mack. 1986. *A causal analysis of learner characteristics and second-language proficiency.* Paper presented at the TESOL Convention, Anaheim, California.

Bachman, L. F. and A. S. Palmer. 1981. The construct validation of the FSI oral interview. *Language Learning* 31: 67–86.

Bachman, L. F. and A. S. Palmer. 1982. The construct validation of some components of communicative proficiency. *TESOL Quarterly* 16(4): 449–65.

Bachman, L. F. and A. S. Palmer. 1983. Basic concerns in test validation. In A. S. Read (Ed.) *Directions in language testing.* Anthology Series 9. Singapore: Singapore University Press.

Bachman, L. F. and A. S. Palmer. 1989. The construct validation of self-ratings of communicative language ability. *Language Testing* 6: 14–29.

Bechtold, H. P. 1959. Construct validity: A critique. *American Psychologist* 14: 619–29.

Bentler, P. M. 1978. The interdependence of theory, methodology, and empirical data: Causal modeling as an approach to construct validation. In D. B. Kandel (Ed.) *Longitudinal research on drug use* (pp. 267–302). Washington D.C.: Hemisphere Publishing Corporation.

Bentler, P.M. 1980. Multivariate analysis with latent variables: Causal modeling. *Annual Review of Psychology* 31:419–56.

Bentler, P. M. 1986. Structural modeling and *Psychometrika*: An historical perspective on growth and achievements. *Psychometrika* 51(1): 35–51.

Bentler, P. M. 1989. *EQS: Structural equations program manual.* Los Angeles: BMDP Statistical Software.

Bentler, P. M. 1990. Comparative fit indexes in structural models. *Psychological Bulletin* 107: 238–46

Bentler, P. M. and D. G. Bonett. 1980. Significance tests and goodness of fit in the analysis of covariance structures. *Psychological Bulletin* 88: 586–606.

Berk, R. A. (Ed.) 1982. *Handbook of methods for detecting test bias.* Baltimore: The Johns Hopkins University Press.

Boldt, R. F. 1988. Latent structure analysis of the TOEFL. *TOEFL Research Reports* 28. Princeton: Educational Testing Service.

Bollen, K. A. 1989. *Structural equations with latent variables.* New York: John Wiley.

Bollen, K. A. and J. S. Long. 1993. *Testing structural equation models.* Newbury Park: Sage.

Boomsma, A. 1987. The robustness of maximum likelihood estimation in structural equation models. In P. Cuttance and R. Ecob (Eds.) *Structural modeling by example* (pp.160–88). Cambridge: Cambridge University Press.

Briere, E. J. 1968. Testing ESL among Navajo children. In J. A. Upshur and J. Fata (Eds.) Problems in foreign language testing. *Language Learning, Special Issue* 3: 11–21.

Briere, E. J. 1973. Cross cultural bias in language testing. In J. W. Oller Jr. and J. Richards (Eds.) *Focus on the learner: Pragmatic perspectives for the language teacher* (pp. 214–27). Rowley: Newbury House.

Briere, E. J. and R. H. Brown. 1971. Norming tests of ESL among Amerindian children. *TESOL Quarterly* 5: 327–34.

Buck, G. 1989. *A construct validation study in listening and reading comprehension*. Paper presented at the 10th Language Testing Research Colloquium, San Antonio, Texas.

Campbell, D. T. 1960. Recommendations for APA test standards regarding construct, trait, or discriminant validity. *American Psychologist* 15: 546–53.

Campbell, D. T. and D. W. Fiske. 1959. Convergent and discriminant validity in the multitrait–multimethod matrix. *Psychological Bulletin* 56: 81–105.

Canale, M. 1983. On some dimensions in language proficiency. In J. W. Oller Jr. (Ed.) *Issues in language testing research* (pp. 333–42). Rowley: Newbury House.

Canale, M. 1988. The measurement of communicative competence. In R. B. Kaplan (Ed.) *Annual Review of Applied Linguistics* 8: 67–84.

Canale, M. and M. Swain. 1980. Theoretical bases of communicative approaches to second language teaching and testing. *Applied Linguistics* 1(1): 1–47.

Carroll, J. B. 1961. The nature of data, or how to choose a correlation coefficient. *Psychometrika* 26: 347–72.

Carroll, J. B. 1962. The prediction of success in foreign language training. In R. Glaser (Ed.) *Training, research and education*. Pittsburg: Pittsburg Press.

Carroll, J. B. 1968. The psychology of language testing. In A. Davies (Ed.) *Language testing symposium. A psycholinguistic perspective* (pp. 46–69). London: Oxford University Press.

Carroll, J. B. 1983. Psychometric theory and language testing. In J. W. Oller Jr. (Ed.) *Issues in language testing research*. Rowley: Newbury House.

Chapelle, C. 1988. Field independence: A source of language test variance? *Language Testing* 5: 62–8.

Chen, Z. and G. Henning. 1985. Linguistic and cultural bias in language proficiency tests. *Language Testing* 2: 155–63.

Chou, C-P., P. M. Bentler and A. Satorra. 1989. *Scaled test statistics and robust standard errors for nonnormal data in covariance structure analysis: A Monte Carlo study*. Paper presented at the American Educational Research Association meeting, San Francisco, California.

Churchman, C. W. 1971. *The design of inquiring systems: Basic concepts of systems and organization*. New York: Basic Books.

Clement, R. 1980. Ethnicity, contact and communicative competence in a second language. In H. Giles, W. P. Robinson and P. M. Smith (Eds.) *Language: Social psychological perspectives*. Oxford: Pergamon.

Clement, R. and B. G. Kruidenier. 1985. Aptitude, attitude and motivation in second language proficiency: A test of Clement's model. *Journal of Language and Social Psychology* 4: 21–37.

Clifford, R. T. 1978. Reliability and validity of language aspects contributing to oral proficiency of prospective teachers of German. In J. L. D. Clark (Ed.) *Direct testing of speaking proficiency: Theory and application* (pp. 191–209). Princeton: Educational Testing Service.

Cooper, R. L. 1968. An elaborated language testing model. In J. A. Upshur and J. Fata (Eds.) Problems in foreign language testing. *Language Learning, Special Issue Number* 3: 15–72.

Cronbach, L. J. 1971. Test validation. In R. L. Thorndike (Ed.) *Educational measurement* (2nd Edn., pp. 443–507). Washington D.C.: American Council on Education.

Cronbach, L. J. 1989. Construct validation after thirty years. In R. L. Linn (Ed.) *Intelligence: Measurement, theory, and public policy* (pp. 147–71). Urbana: University of Illinois Press.

Cronbach, L. J. and P. E. Meehl. 1955. Construct validity in psychological tests. *Psychological Bulletin* 52: 281–302.

Cross, T. 1977. Mother's speech adjustments: The contribution of selected child listener variables. In C. Snow and C. Ferguson *Talking to children* (pp. 151–88). Cambridge: Cambridge University Press.

Cummins, J. and M. Swain. 1986. *Bilingualism in education.* New York: Longman.

Cuttance, P. 1987. Issues and problems in the applications of structural equation models. In P. Cuttance and R. Ecob (Eds.), *Structural modeling by example* (pp. 241–79). Cambridge: Cambridge University Press.

Davidson, F. G. 1988. *An exploratory modeling survey of the trait structures of some existing language test data sets.* Unpublished Ph.D. dissertation. Los Angeles, University of California.

Delandshere, G. 1986. *Structural equation modeling applied to multilevel data: The effect of teaching practices on eighth-grade mathematics achievement.* Unpublished Ph.D. dissertation. Los Angeles, University of California.

Dulay, H. C. and M. K. Burt. 1978. *Why bilingual education? A summary of findings* (2nd Edn.). San Francisco: Bloomsbury West.

Dulay, H. C., M. K. Burt and S. D. Krashen. 1982. *Language two.* New York: Oxford University Press.

Dunbar, S. 1982. *Construct validity and the internal structure of a foreign language test for several native language groups.* Paper presented at the American Educational Research Association, New York.

Ecob, R. 1987. Applications of structural equation modeling to longitudinal educational data. In P. Cuttance and R. Ecob (Eds.) *Structural modeling by example* (pp. 138–59). Cambridge: Cambridge University Press.

Ecob, R. and P. Cuttance. 1987. An overview of structural equation modeling. In P. Cuttance and R. Ecob (Eds.) *Structural modeling by example* (pp. 9–23). Cambridge: Cambridge University Press.

Embretson, S. 1983. Construct validity: Construct representation versus nomothetic span. *Psychological Bulletin* 93: 179–97.

Farhady, H. 1979. The disjunctive fallacy between discrete-point and integrative tests. *TESOL Quarterly* 13: 347–58.

Feyerabend, P. 1975. *Against method.* London: New Left Books.

Feyerabend, P. 1981. *Problems of empiricism: Philosophical papers.* Volume 2. Cambridge: Cambridge University Press.

Fouly, K. 1985. *A confirmatory multivariate study of the nature of second language proficiency and its relationships to learner variables.* Unpublished Ph.D. dissertation. Urbana, University of Illinois.

Fouly, K., L. F. Bachman and G. A. Cziko. 1990. The divisibility of language competence: A confirmatory approach. *Language Learning* 40: 1–21.

Freed, B. 1980. Talking to foreigners versus talking to children. In R. Scarcella and S. D. Krashen. (Eds.) *Research in second language acquisition* (pp. 19–27). Rowley: Newbury House.

Freedman, D. A. 1987. As others see us: A case study in path analysis. *Journal of Educational Statistics* 12: 101–28.

French, J. W. 1965. The relationship of problem-solving styles to the factor composition of tests. *Educational and Psychological Measurement* 25: 9–28.

Gaies, S. 1977. The nature of linguistic input in formal second language learning: Linguistic and communicative strategies in ESL teachers' classroom language. In H. D. Brown, C. Yorio and R. Crymes, *On TESOL '77* (pp. 204–12). Washington D.C.: TESOL.

Gardner, R. C. 1979. Social psychological aspects of second language acquisition. In H. Giles and R. St. Clair (Eds.) *Language and social psychology* (pp. 193–220). Oxford: Blackwell.

Gardner, R. C. 1985. *Social psychology and second language learning: The role of attitudes and motivation.* London: Edward Arnold.

Gardner, R. C. 1988. The socio-educational model of second language learning: Assumptions, findings and issues. *Language Learning* 38: 101–26.

Gardner, R. C. and R. Clement. 1990. Social psychological perspectives on second language acquisition. In H. Giles and W. P. Robinson (Eds.) *Handbook of language and social psychology* (pp. 495–517). New York: John Wiley.

Gardner, R. C., R. N. Lalonde, R. Moorcraft and F. T. Evers. 1987. Second language attrition: The role of motivation and use. *Journal of Language and Social Psychology* 6: 1–47.

Gardner, R. C., R. N. Lalonde and R. Pierson. 1983. The socio-educational model of second language acquisition: An investigation using LISREL causal modeling. *Journal of Language and Social Psychology* 2: 1–15.

Gardner, R. C. and W. E. Lambert. 1959. Motivation variables in second language acquisition. *Canadian Journal of Psychology* 13: 266–72.

Gardner, R.C. and W. E. Lambert. 1972. *Attitudes and motivation in second language learning.* Rowley: Newbury House.

Gardner, R. C. and L. M. Lysynchuk (in press). The role of aptitude, attitudes, motivation and language use on second–language acquisition and retention. *Canadian Journal of Behaviourial Sciences.*

Gardner, R. C., P. C. Smythe, R. Clement and L. Gliksman. 1976. Second language learning: A social psychological perspective. *Canadian Modern Language Review* 32: 198–213.

Giles, H. and J. L. Byrne. 1982. An intergroup approach to second language acquisition. *Journal of Multilingual and Multicultural Development,* 1, 17–40.

Gustafsson, J-E. and G. Balke (in press). General and specific abilities as predictors of social achievement. *Multivariate Behavioral Research.*

Hale, G. A., D. A. Rock and T. Jirele. 1989. Confirmatory factor analysis of the Test of English as a Foreign Language. *TOEFL Research Reports 32.* Princeton: Educational Testing Service.

Halliday, M. A. K. and R. Hasan. 1976. *Cohesion in English.* London: Longman.

Hansen, L. and C. Stansfield. 1984. Field dependence-independence and language testing: Evidence from six Pacific-Island cultures. *TESOL Quarterly* 18: 311–24.

Harley, B., J. P. B. Allen, J. Cummins and M. Swain. 1987. *The development of bilingual proficiency: Final report.* Toronto: Ontario: Modern Language Centre, Ontario Institute for Studies in Education.

Harris, D. P. 1969. *Testing English as a second language.* New York: McGraw-Hill.

Hendricks, D., G. Scholz, R. Spurling, M. Johnson and L. Vandenburg. 1980. Oral proficiency testing in an intensive English language program. In J. W. Oller Jr. and K. Perkins (Eds.) *Research in language testing* (pp. 77–90). Rowley: Newbury House.

Hill, P. W. 1987. Modeling the hierarchical structure of learning. In P. Cuttance and R. Ecob (Eds.) *Structural modeling by example* (pp. 65–85). Cambridge: Cambridge University Press.

Hinofotis, F. 1983. The structure of oral communication in an educational environment: A comparison of factor analytical rotation procedures. In J. W. Oller Jr. (Ed.) *Issues in language testing research* (pp. 170–87). Rowley: Newbury House.

Hisama, K. K. 1980. An analysis of various ESL proficiency tests. In J. W. Oller Jr. and K. Perkins (Eds.) *Research in language testing* (pp. 47–53). Rowley: Newbury House.

Holland, P. W. and H. Wainer. 1993. *Differential item functioning.* Hillsdale: Lawrence Erlbaum Associates.

Hymes, D. H. 1972. On communicative competence. In J. B. Pride and J. Holmes (Eds.) *Sociolinguistics* (pp. 269–93). Harmondsworth: Penguin.

Hymes, D. H. 1973. Toward linguistic competence. *Texas Working Papers in Sociolinguistics, Working Paper No.16.* Austin: Center for Intercultural Studies in Communication and Department of Anthropology, University of Texas.

James, L.R., S.A. Mulaik and J.M. Brett. 1982. *Causal analysis: Assumptions, models and data.* Beverly Hills, CA: Sage.

Johnson, T. R. and K. Krug. 1980. Integrative and instrumental motivations in search of a measure. In J. W. Oller Jr. and K. Perkins (Eds.) *Research in language testing* (pp. 241–49). Rowley: Newbury House.

Jones, W. R. 1941. The attitudes of central school pupils to certain school subjects and the correlation between attitude and attainment. *British Journal of Educational Psychology* 11: 28–44.

Jones, W. R. 1950. Attitude towards Welsh as a second language: A further investigation. *British Journal of Educational Psychology* 20: 117–32.

Joreskog, K. G. and D. Sorbom. 1979. *Advances in factor analysis and structural equation models.* Cambridge, MA: Abt Books.

Joreskog, K. G. and D. Sorbom. 1984. *LISREL VI, User's guide.* Chicago: National Educational Resources.

Krashen, S. D. 1985. *The input hypothesis.* London: Longman.

Kunnan, A. J. 1990. Differential item functioning and native language and gender groups: The case of an ESL placement examination. *TESOL Quarterly* 24: 741–6.

Kunnan, A. J. 1992. An investigation of a criterion-referenced test using G-theory, and factor and cluster analysis. *Language Testing* 9: 30-49.

Kunnan, A.J. 1994. Modelling relationships among some test-taker characteristics and performance on EFL tests: An approach to construct validation. *Language Testing* 11: 225-52.

Lado, R. 1961. *Language testing.* New York: McGraw-Hill.

Lambert, W. E. 1963. Psychological approaches to the study of language 1: On learning, thinking and human abilities. *Modern Language Journal* 14: 51–62.

Lambert, W. E. 1967. A social psychology of bilingualism. *Journal of Social Issues* 23: 91–109.

Lansman, M. and E. Hunt. 1980. *Individual differences in secondary task performance* (NR 154–398 ONR Technical Report No.7). Department of Psychology. Seattle: University of Washington.

Laosa, L. M. 1991. The cultural context of construct validity and the ethics of generalizability. Research Report. Princeton: Educational Testing Service.

Loevinger, J. 1957. Objective tests as instruments of psychological theory. *Psychological Reports* 3: 635–94.

Messick, S. 1980. Test validity and the ethics of assessment. *American Psychologist* 35: 1012–27.

Messick, S. 1989. Validity. In R. L. Linn (Ed.) *Educational measurement* (3rd Edn., pp. 13–103). New York: American Council on Education.

Munby, J. 1978. *Communicative syllabus design.* Cambridge: Cambridge University Press.

Murakami, M. 1980. Behavioral and attitudinal correlates of progress in ESL by native speakers of Japanese. In J. W. Oller Jr. and K. Perkins (Eds.) *Research in language testing* (pp. 227–32). Rowley: Newbury House.

Muthen, B. 1987. *LISCOMP: Analysis of linear structural equations with a comprehensive measurement model* (Users's Guide). Moorsville: Scientific Software.

Muthen, B. 1988. Some uses of structural equation modeling in validity studies: Extending IRT to external variables. In H. Wainer and H. Braun (Eds.) *Test Validity* (pp. 213–38). Hillside: Lawrence Erlbaum.

Muthen, B. 1989a. Latent variable modeling in heterogenous populations. *Psychometrika* 54: 557–85.

Muthen, B. 1989b. Factor structure in groups selected on observed scores. *British Journal of Mathematical and Statistical Psychology* 42: 81–90.

Naiman, N., M. Frohlich, H. H. Stern and A. Todesco. 1978. *The good language learner.* Research in Education series 7. Ontario Institute for Studies in Education.

Nation, R. and B. McLaughlin. 1986. Experts and novices: An information processing approach to the "good language learner" problem. *Applied Psycholinguistics* 7: 41–56.

Nelson, F. H., R. G. Lomax and R. Perlman. 1984. A structural equation model of second language acquisition of adult learners. *Journal of Experimental Education* 53: 29–39.

Newport, E., H. Gleitman and L. Gleitman. 1977. Mother, I'd rather do it myself: Some effects and non-effects of maternal speech style. In C. Snow and C. Ferguson,*Talking to children* (pp. 109–49). Cambridge: Cambridge University Press.

Oller, J. W. Jr. 1972. Scoring methods and difficulty levels for cloze tests of proficiency in ESL. *Modern Language Journal* 56: 151–8.

Oller, J. W. Jr. 1976. Evidence of a general language profiency factor: an expectancy grammar. *Die Neuren Sprachen* 76: 165–74

Oller, J. W. Jr. 1979. *Language tests at school.* London: Longman.

Oller, J. W. Jr. 1983. Evidence for a general language proficiency factor: An expectancy grammar. In J. W. Oller (Ed.) *Issues in language testing research.* Rowley: Newbury House.

Oller, J. W. Jr. and F. Hinofotis. 1980. Two mutually exclusive hypotheses about second language ability: Indivisible or partially divisible competence. In J. W. Oller Jr. and K. Perkins (Eds.) *Research in language testing.* Rowley: Newbury House.

Oller, J. W. Jr., K. Perkins and M. Murakami. 1980. Seven types of variables in relation to ESL learning. In J. W. Oller Jr. and K. Perkins (Eds.) *Research in language testing* (pp. 233–40). Rowley: Newbury House.

Oltman, P. K., L. J. Stricker and T. Barrows. 1988. Native language, English proficiency, and the structure of the TOEFL. *TOEFL Research Reports 27.* Princeton: Educational Testing Service.

O'Malley, J. M., A. U. Chamot, G. Stewner-Manzares, L. Kupper and R. P. Russo. 1985. Learning strategies used by beginning and intermediate ESL students. *Language Learning* 33. 21–46.

Pena-Taveras, M. S. and A. B. Cambel. 1989. Nonlinear, stochastic model for energy investment in manufacturing. *Energy – The International Journal*, 14, 421-33.

Popper, K. R. 1962. *Conjectures and refutations: The growth of scientific knowledge.* New York: Harper and Row.

Purcell, E. T. 1983. Models of pronunciation accuracy. In J. W. Oller (Ed.) *Issues in language testing research* (pp. 133–53). Rowley: Newbury House.

Quine, W. V. O. 1953. Two dogmas of Empiricism. In *From a Logical Point of View*, Chapter 2. Cambridge, MA.:Harvard University Press.

Rindskopf, D. and T. Rose. 1988. Some theory and applications of confirmatory second-order factor analysis. *Multivariate Behavioral Research*, 23, 51-67.

Rose, A. M. 1978. *An information processing approach to performance assessment* (NR 150–391 ONR Final Technical Report). Washington D.C.: American Institutes for Research.

Rubin, J. 1981. Study of cognitive processes in second language learning. *Applied Linguistics* 2: 117–31.

Sang, F., B. Schmitz, H. J. Vollmer, J. Baumert and P. M. Roeder. 1986. Models of second language competence: A structural equation approach. *Language Testing* 3: 54–79.

Saris, W.E., J. den Ronden and A. Satorra. 1987. Testing structural equation models. In P. Cuttance and R. Ecob (Eds.) *Structural modeling by example* (pp. 202–20). Cambridge: Cambridge University Press.

Sasaki, M. 1991. *Relationships among second language proficiency, foreign language aptitude, and intelligence: A structural equation modeling approach.* Unpublished Ph.D. dissertation. Los Angeles, University of California.

Satorra, A. and P. M. Bentler. 1988a. *Scaling corrections for statistics in covariance structure analysis.* Los Angeles: UCLA Statistics Series # 2.

Satorra, A. and P. M. Bentler, 1988b. Scaling corrections for chi-square statistics in covariance structure analysis. *Proceedings of the American Statistical Association,* 308–13.

Scholz, G., D. Hendricks, R. Spurling, M. Johnson and L. Vandenburg. 1980. Is language ability divisible or unitary? A factor analysis of 22 English language proficiency tests. In J. W. Oller Jr. and K. Perkins (Eds.) *Research in language testing.* Rowley: Newbury House.

Schumann, J. 1978. The acculturation model for second language acquisition. In R. Gringas (Ed.) *Second language acquisition and foreign language teaching.* Arlington: Center for Applied Linguistics.

Schumann, J. 1993. Some problems with falsification: An illustration from SLA research. *Applied Linguistics*, 14: 295-306.

Shohamy, E. 1983. The stability of oral proficiency assessment on the oral interview testing procedure. *Language Learning* 33: 527–40.

Shohamy, E. 1984. Does the testing method make a difference? The case of reading comprehension. *Language Testing* 1: 147–70.

Skehan, P. 1989. *Individual differences in second-language learning.* London: Edward Arnold.

Skehan, P. 1991. Individual differences in second language learning. *Studies in Second Language Acquisition* 13: 275–98.

Stage, F. K. 1990. LISREL: An introduction and applications in higher education research. In J. Smart (Ed.) *Higher education handbook of theory and research,* 6. New York: Agathon Press.

Stansfield, C. and J. Hansen 1983. Field dependence–independence as a variable in second language cloze test performance. *TESOL Quarterly* 17: 29–38.

Swinton, S. S. and D. E. Powers. 1980. Factor analysis of the TOEFL. *TOEFL Research Report* 6. Princeton: Educational Testing Service.

Turner, C. E. 1989. The underlying factor structure of L2 cloze test performance in francophone, university–level students: Causal modeling as an approach to construct validation. *Language Testing* 6: 172-97.

University of Cambridge Local Examinations Syndicate (UCLES). 1987. *English as a foreign language: General handbook.* Cambridge: University of Cambridge Local Examinations Syndicate.

Upshur, J. A. 1983. Measurement of individual differences and explanation in the language sciences. *Language Learning* 33: 99–140.

Upshur, J. A. and T. J. Homburg. 1983. Some relations among tests at successive ability levels. In J. W. Oller Jr. (Ed.) *Issues in language testing research.* Rowley: Newbury House.

Van Lier, L. (in press) Forks and hope: Pursuing understanding in different ways. *Applied Linguistics.*

Vernon, P. A., D. N. Jackson and S. Messick. 1986. Cultural influences on patterns of abilities in North America. *Research Report* 41. Princeton: Educational Testing Service.

Vollmer, H. J., and F. Sang. 1983. Competing hypotheses about second language ability: A plea for caution. In J. W. Oller Jr. (Ed.) *Issues in language testing research.* Rowley: Newbury House.

Wang, L-S. 1988. *A comparative analysis of cognitive achievement and psychological orientation among language minority groups: A linear structural relations (LISREL) approach.* Unpublished Ph.D. dissertation. Urbana, University of Illinois.

Welch, C., A. Doolittle and J. McLarty. 1989. Differential performance on a direct measure of writing skills for black and white college freshman. *ACT Research Report Series,* 8. Iowa City: American College Testing Program.

West, B. J. and J. Salk. 1987. Complexity, organizations, and uncertainty. *European Journal of Operational Research* 30: 117–28.

Wheaton, B. 1987. Assessment of fit in over-identified models with latent variables. *Sociological Methods and Research* 16: 118–54.

Wheaton, B., B. Muthen, D. F. Alwin and G. F. Summers. 1977. Assessing reliability and stability in panel models. In D. R. Heise (Ed.) *Sociological Methodology 1977* (pp. 84–136). San Francisco: Jossey Bass.

Widdowson, H. G. 1978. *Teaching language as communication.* Oxford: Oxford University Press.

Wittgenstein, L. 1922. *Tractatus logico-philosophicus.* Translated by Pears and McGuiness. London: Routledge and Kegan Paul.

Zeidner, M. 1986. Are English language aptitude tests biased towards culturally different minority groups? Some Israeli findings. *Language Testing* 3: 80–98.

Zeidner, M. 1987. A comparison of ethnic, sex and age bias in the predictive validity of English language aptitude tests: Some Israeli data. *Language Testing* 4: 55–71.

Subject Index

A

Acquisition 5, 7, 13–15, 17–18, 75
Affective filter 14
Age 25
Aptitude 18
Attitude 18, 20, 21

B

Background knowledge 8
Bentler–Bonett nonnormed fit index 30, 31
Bentler–Bonett normed fit index 30, 31
Bi–factor model 52

C

Causal–modeling 3, 5
Communicative language ability 8, 11, 12
Comparative fit index 31, 62, 69, 77
Comprehensible input 14, 15
Confirmatory factor analysis 24
Construct validity/validation 1, 2–5, 7, 11, 38, 41, 78, 81
Content analysis 2, 77
Convergent validation 2, 5
Culture/Cultural background 8, 17
Culture–fair tests 17

D

Dependent variables 13–14, 20
Differential item functioning 17

E

Ecological generalizability 9
EQS 7, 9, 19, 28, 29, 53, 79
Equal influence factors model 44–45, 57, 71, 77

Exploratory factor analysis 6, 10, 19, 23, 24, 35, 37, 41, 42, 48, 51, 52, 54, 70, 76

F
Factor analysis 6, 15, 19, 35, 37, 41, 48, 51, 52, 54, 70, 76, 77, 78, 79
FCE Paper 1 26, 27–8, 37–8, 47, 74, 76
FCE Paper 2 26, 27–8, 37–8, 47, 74, 76
FCE Paper 3 26, 27–8, 37–8, 47, 74, 76
FCE Paper 4 27–8, 37–8, 47, 76
FCE Paper 5 27–8, 37–8, 47, 76
First Certificate in English 9, 10, 25, 26–27, 28, 73

G
G–factor 15
Gardner's intervening factors model 45–6, 62, 71, 77
Generalizability 9–10, 17, 34
Generalizability boundaries 17

H
Higher–order general factor 51, 52, 54, 70, 75

I
Independent variables 13, 20, 30
Individual difference variables 16, 45
Individual differences 4, 13, 14, 81
Input hypothesis 14, 15, 17, 18
Intelligence 1, 10, 13, 14, 15, 45
Intervening factors model 14, 45, 46, 62, 71, 77

K
Kantian inquiry system 4–5

L
Lagrange Multiplier Test 31, 57, 63
Language achievement 7, 18, 20, 21
Latent or unobserved variables 19, 20
LISCOMP 19, 29, 79, 80
LISREL 7, 19, 20, 29, 79

M
Modeling 1, 2–6, 7, 9, 11, 19, 20–2, 24, 41, 48–71, 72, 75–6, 77–8, 79, 80–1, 82

Monitor 14, 15, 18, 43, 75
Monitoring 18–19, 26, 33, 36, 41, 43, 45, 61, 62, 63, 75
Motivation 1, 4, 8, 18, 20, 26, 33, 36, 41, 45, 77, 81

N
Native language 1, 6, 15, 17, 26, 38, 72, 81
Nested factor model 52, 53, 70, 71, 76
Nomological network 2, 3, 5
Nomothetic span 3–6, 81

O
Observed variables 9, 19, 20

P
Personal attributes 5, 6, 7, 8, 78, 81
Population generalizability 9, 17
Pronunciation 16, 18, 28, 76

R
Random measurement error 5, 11, 13

S
Satorra and Bentler scaled test 31, 49, 56, 64
SPEAK 9, 10, 26–7, 28, 34, 37, 39, 47, 73, 76, 77

T
Task generalizability 10
Temporal generalizability 9
Test bias 17
Test method facets 5, 8, 78, 80
Test of English as a Foreign Language 9, 10, 16, 26–7, 28, 37–8, 47, 73, 76
Test of English Writing 9, 10, 26–7, 28, 37–8, 47, 73, 76
Test of Spoken English 9, 26–7, 37–38

U
Unitary trait hypothesis 15

W
Wald test 31–2, 57, 58, 63

Author Index

A

Allen, J.P.B.   14
Alwin, D.F.   20, 30
Ayer, A.J.   2

B

Bachman, L. F.   1, 5, 7, 8, 9, 11, 12, 13, 15, 16, 18, 20, 22, 23, 24, 25, 29, 33, 34, 37, 38, 51, 52, 54, 70, 75, 76, 77, 78, 80
Balke, G.   52, 70, 76
Barrows, T.   17
Baumert, J.   5, 15
Bechtold, H.P.   2
Bentler, P.M.   2, 3, 4, 9, 19, 24, 28, 30, 31, 49, 56, 59, 64, 77
Berk, R.A.   17
Boldt, R.F.   5
Bollen, K.A.   19, 57
Bonett, D. G.   30, 49, 56, 59, 64
Boomsma, A.   52
Briere, E.J.   17
Brown, R.H.   17
Buck, G.   16
Burt, M.K.   14, 23
Byrne, J.L.   14, 18

C

Cambel, A.B.   82
Campbell, D.T.   2, 3
Canale, M.   8, 11
Carroll, J.B.   8, 12, 13, 14, 15
Chamot, A.U.   18
Chapelle, C.   7
Chen, Z.   17
Choi, I-C.   9, 16, 24, 25, 33, 34, 37, 38, 51, 52, 54, 70, 76
Chou, C-P.   30
Churchman, C.W.   4, 5

Clement, R.   14, 16, 18, 19, 29
Clifford, R.T.   16
Cooper, R.L.   12
Cronbach, L. J.   1, 2, 3, 5, 6, 78
Cross, T.   18
Cummins, J.   14
Cuttance, P.   19, 30, 31
Cziko, G.A.   16

D

Davidson, F. G.   9, 13, 15, 16, 24, 25, 33, 34, 37, 38, 51, 52, 54, 70, 76, 80
Delandshere, G.   19
Doolittle, A.   17
Dulay, H.C.   14, 23
Dunbar, S.   16

E

Ecob, R.   18, 19
Embretson, S.   3, 4, 5
Evers, F. T.   19, 20

F

Farhady, H.   17
Feyerabend, P.   5
Fiske, D.W.   2
Foulkes, J.   15
Fouly, K.   7, 16, 18, 19, 23
Freed, B.   18
Freedman, D.A.   23, 70
French, J.W.   6
Frohlich, M.   13, 15, 18

G

Gaies, S.   18
Gardner, R.C.   1, 7, 8, 14, 15, 16, 18, 19, 20, 21, 22, 29, 45, 62, 71, 77, 79
Giles, H.   14, 18, 79
Gleitman, H.   18
Gleitman, L.   18
Gliksman, L.   18
Gustafsson, J-E.   52, 70, 76

H

Hale, G.A.   5, 16
Halliday, M. A. K.   8
Hansen, J.   7
Hansen, L.   7
Harley, B.   14
Harris, D.P.   12
Hasan, R.   8
Hendricks, D.   15
Henning, G.   17
Hill, P.W.   19
Hinofotis, F.   5, 15, 16
Hisama, K.K.   15
Holland, P.W.   17
Homburg, T.J.   15
Hunt, E.   80
Hymes, D.H.   8, 11

J

Jackson, D.N.   17
James   4
Jirele, T.   5, 16
Johnson, M.   15
Johnson, T.R.   18
Jones, W.R.   18
Joreskog, K.G.   4, 19, 20, 29, 30

K

Krashen, S.D.   8, 14, 15, 17, 18, 43, 75
Krug, K.   18
Kruidenier, B.G.   14, 19, 29
Kunnan, A.J.   13, 15, 17, 19
Kupper, L.   18

L

Lado, R.   8, 12
Lalonde, R.N.   19, 20
Lambert, W.E.   8, 14, 18
Lansman, M.   80
Laosa, L.M.   17, 38, 41
Loevinger, J.   2
Lomax, R.G.   19

Long, J.S.   19
Lynch, B.   80
Lysynchuk, L.M.   18

M
Mack, M.   18
McLarty, J.   17
McLaughlin, B.   74
Meehl, P.E.   2, 3, 5
Messick, S.   2, 3, 4, 5, 17
Milanovic, M.   13, 80
Moorcraft, R.   19, 20
Munby, J.   11
Murakami, M.   18
Muthen, B.   19, 20, 29, 30, 80, 81

N
Naiman, N.   13, 15, 18
Nation, R.   74
Nelson, F.H.   19
Newport, E.   18

O
Oller, J.W.   5, 15, 16, 18
Oltman, P.K.   17
O'Malley, J.M.   18

P
Palmer, A.S.   5, 7, 15, 16, 29, 54
Pena-Taveras, M.S.   82
Perkins, K.   18
Perlman, R.   19
Pierson, R.   19
Popper, K.R.   2
Powers, D.E.   15
Purcell, E.T.   16

Q
Quine, W.V.O.   5

R
Rindskopf, D.   52
Rock, D.A.   5, 16

Roeder, P. M.   3, 13
Ronden, J. den 30
Rose, A.M.   80
Rose, T. 52
Rubin, J.   18
Russo, R.P.   18
Ryan, K.   9, 16, 24, 25, 33, 34, 37, 38, 51, 52, 54, 70, 76

S
Salk, J.   82
Sang, F.   5, 15
Saris, W.E.   30
Sasaki, M.   19
Satorra, A.   30, 31, 49, 56, 59, 64
Schmitz, B.   5, 15
Scholz, G.   15
Schumann, J. 5, 13, 15
Shohamy, E.   16
Skehan, P.   5, 6, 14, 77
Smythe, P.C.   18
Sorbom, D.   4, 19, 20, 29, 30
Spurling, R.   15
Stage, F.K.   30
Stansfield, C.   7
Stern, H.H.   13, 15, 18
Stewner-Manzares, G.   18
Stricker, L.J.   17
Summers, G.F.   20, 30
Swain, M.   8, 11, 14
Swinton, S.S.   15

T
Todesco, A.   13, 15, 18
Turner, C.E.   16

U
Upshur, J. A.   15, 81

V
Van Lier, L.   5
Vandenburg, L.   15
Vanniarajan, S.   13

Vernon, P.A.   17
Vollmer, H.J.   5, 15

W
Wainer, H.   17
Wang, L-S.   18, 19, 23
Welch, C.   17
West, B.J.   82
Wheaton, B.   20, 30, 31
Widdowson, H.G.   11
Wittgenstein, L.   2

Z
Zeidner, M.   17